Divining the Future of Africa
Healing the Wounds, Restoring Dignity and Fostering Development

Munyaradzi Mawere

Langaa Research & Publishing CIG
Mankon, Bamenda

Publisher:
Langaa RPCIG
Langaa Research & Publishing Common Initiative Group
P.O. Box 902 Mankon
Bamenda
North West Region
Cameroon
Langaagrp@gmail.com
www.langaa-rpcig.net

Distributed in and outside N. America by African Books Collective
orders@africanbookscollective.com
www.africanbookcollective.com

ISBN: 9956-792-28-4

DISCLAIMER
All views expressed in this publication are those of the author and do not
necessarily reflect the views of Langaa RPCIG.

Dedication

To all concerned citizens of the African continent

Table of Contents

Acknowledgements

With the exception of the introduction, chapters 3, 5, and 6, the other chapters of this book appeared previously in the following journals, but of course with several modifications on the titles and content: 'African cultures and globalisation: The impact of globalisation on the posterity of African cultures with reference to Mozambique, South Africa and Zimbabwe', *Africana Journal of Ideas*, 4 (2), 2010 (chapter 1); 'Decolonising African languages: An unfinished business', *International Journal of English Literature*, 2 (1), 2011 (chapter 2); 'African indigenous knowledge systems and morality: Have African IKS run out of steam?' *Journal of Sustainable Development in Africa*, 12 (7), 2010 (chapter 4). My thanks are due to the publishers for allowing me to reprint the chapters in this book, of course with some modifications in their titles and contents.

I would like also to thank Dr. Samuel Awuah-Nyamekye of the University of Cape Coast, Ghana for his meticulous reading and reviewing of the first draft of the manuscript. I found his comments and suggestions constructive and penetrating. My heartfelt thanks also go to Prof Francis B. Nyamnjoh, one of the Pan-African luminaries of this century, for his longstanding scholarly guidance. May God bless you even more abundantly!

Introduction

Africa, indigenous knowledge systems, development and globalisation

The *Economist* magazine once declared that *"Africa is a hopeless continent"* thereby casting the African continent in a 4D horror of destruction, disease, disaster and disappointment. This is an imagination that in no doubt retards the African people's intellectual emancipation thereby shattering their hopes forever more. It is the same realisation that provoked Kuper (1988) to write his book: *The Invention of Primitive Society* in which he argues that such a construction demanded a projection and imposition of the Westerners' own society and values on other societies such as Africa. A series of mind boggling questions could, therefore, be asked in view of the *Economist's* imagination of Africa: "Is the Economist's imagination of Africa a genuine and correct one that the entire world could trust?" "Is Africa really a hopeless continent?" "In what sense is Africa a hopeless continent?" "If Africa is really a hopeless continent, who is to blame for her hopelessness?" "Considering the sad history that Africa has experienced over the years, could she ever re-imagine herself as a *hopeful* continent?" These and many other critical questions trouble contemporary scholars and theorists interested in the future of Africa, especially understanding her geopolitics and socio-economic situation.

I have chosen to start this book with an imagination of the African continent by the *Economist* because the present text seeks to re-imagine the same continent whose future was once imagined beyond despair. I seek to re-imagine the future of Africa because I see a lot of biases in the *Economist's* imagination as it conceals more facts and realities about Africa than it reveals especially economic-wise. In fact, after Africa's subjugation by the imperial countries of Europe through slavery and colonialism, the hope for the continent could only be found in the independence of Africa and the people of Africa both on the continent and beyond. Yet, while it is true that colonial administrations have since vacated the African soils, the recent tide of globalisation, which indeed, is more of the imposition of Euro-American culture and values on the continent, Africa, especially its indigenous knowledge systems remain far from being independent: the nefarious ghost of Europe and America continue to haunt the innocent continent of Africa. Africa's pool of indigenous knowledge systems which in fact is the backbone of the continent's moral and education systems, conservational practices and political as well as socio-economic development remain submerged in the labyrinths and cobwebs of confusion, leaving the continent suffering from cultural, political, and socio-economic amnesia.

A cursory look at southern African education system proves this point beyond doubt: that the present tide of globalisation is determined to wipe away from the scene all the African residual cultural norms and values. In most if not all southern African education systems, the language of the former colonial master which are indeed foreign to the learners and their experiences remain dominant or rather the language of instruction. In countries like Zimbabwe, South Africa, Zambia, Malawi and many others, English, for example, remains the dominant language of instruction in schools and even in job markets. In Mozambique, Portuguese continue enjoying the same privilege several decades after the demise of the Portuguese colonial rule in the country. This entails that while colonial administration has since vacated the African soil the former colonialists' 'invisible hands' or what I consider as the 'notorious ghost of colonialism' continues to haunt African learners in the education institutions.

On the moral side, there is ample evidence that since the dawn of colonialism, Africa's moral values have not only been eroded but despised by the colonial architects. I have argued elsewhere (Mawere 2012; 2013; 2014) that the relegation of African moral values as null and void started immediate after the advent of colonialism and its hegemonic tendencies over Africa. In view of the Western colonialism's hegemonic culture, I follow Ranajit Guha (1997: 23) in using the term *hegemony* to refer to 'a condition of dominance, such that, in the organic composition of dominance, persuasion outweighs coercion'. The missionaries had to castigate African thought and moral values in order for their Western values to gain acceptance and prominence over the local ones. Anything perceived African, from medicine to philosophical thought, religion to moral thought, and socio-economical to political systems were all castigated while everything perceived Western was embraced, cherished and preached as civilised and the best of all values. In the new schools and churches, only Western moral values were preached as the only correct ones and the new converts encouraged by the missionaries to embrace these [values] without question but despise and question any value associated with their traditional African way of life. This type of outlook could possibly lead to 'authoritarian moralism' (Wiredu 1996).This is because the 'missionaries often claimed universalism and superiority for their own moral principles ... and they [missionaries] sometimes sought to impose their own customs on Africans in the aggressive conviction that they were moral principles' (Wiredu 1996: 200).

I should be quick here to stress that this way of doing have not ended with the demise of colonialism, and in particular the disappearance of colonial administration in Africa. It has continued even after colonialism through those Africans who have been brainwashed and remained mentally colonised and Euro-American scholars and theorists who still strongly feel that people of European and American descent are more superior to those from the other parts of the world. Academics being the mouth-pieces of many social movements, Euro-American scholars have continued eulogising Euro-American values and castigating to oblivion those of other cultures across the world. This has been perpetuated in the name of globalisation which on the African continent has largely been a replacement of African values by those that are Euro-American. Such a scenario as this is more visible in education curricula in many African countries where languages of former colonialists (such as English and Portuguese), syllabuses, and extra-curriculum activities (such as rugby, tennis ball, etc.) remain at the centre of the education systems. In the case of the latter, for example, this is in spite of the fact that most of the African traditional games had (and continue to have) moral values embedded in them (see Mawere 2012).

The same remains true for other areas like conservation (of both resources and the environment). During colonialism, local conservation strategies were despised and labelled as irrational, superstitious and unscientific. With this move by the colonial administrators, Africans were forced to abandon their indigenous knowledge related to conservation as those that were foreign were made to set in. On realising that with the end of colonialism in Africa, people were likely to go back to their 'old ways' – traditional conservation strategies – the West had to come in the guise of externally initiated community-based natural resource management (CBNRM) which was mainly instituted through the non-governmental organisations and sometimes national government agencies. Like conservation during colonialism, externally initiated CBNRM as opposed to organic CBNRM[1], did not consider the

---

[1] There are three main models of CBNRM namely organic, imposed and assisted models. Organic model, which is the one practised in Norumedzo, are characterised by more collaboration and less competition among stakeholders, common vision, communities inputting into policy processes, knowledge generation, sharing of experience, benefits generation and

contribution and strategies of the local people in the conservation of resources and the environment. They wrongly assumed that the local people are ignorant and can only learn from them as experts. Elsewhere (Mawere 2012; 2014), I have argued that in many parts of Africa, this only extended the environmental crises that started with colonialism as the move repeated the same blunder that the colonial administrators made during their time. It has been proven beyond reasonable doubt by many scholars (Katerere 1999; Marongwe 2004; Mukamuri 1995; Pollard and Cousins 2014; Hoole 2014; Sowman and Wynberg 2014) that where local people do not actively take part and their contributions unrecognised by the external initiators of CBNRM, such projects are likely to collapse. The local people, instead of supporting, will sabotage the initiative. Besides, Western scientific conservation strategies alone, have proven futile since their institution as sole and best practices for conservation. The extension of environmental crises the world-over is clear testimony that Western science alone cannot help to resolve the environmental problems the world is facing today. There is need for complementing strategies such as those from the indigenous knowledge systems of various groups across the world.

All the above is clear testimony that there is urgent need for the reinstitution of 'local' or indigenous methodologies, strategies and epistemologies to complement Western science in all the attempts to ease the tapestry of problems that the

---

sharing among other benefits. Imposed models are marked by fierce competition among stakeholders, lack of common vision, no involvement of communities in policy processes, individualism, no sharing of information, no benefit sharing, conflict between government and local communities and many other factors. Assisted CBNRM models lie between the two extreme models, organic and imposed (see Katerere 1999; Marongwe 2002: 194).

world is suffering from. Continued relegation of indigenous knowledge systems of all forms will do more harm than good, and will certainly extend the problems that the world is experiencing in areas such as morality, politics, economics, education and conservation, among many others.

In view of this realisation, the present book comes at the right time – a time when the talk on the need to embrace knowledge diversity is high on the agenda of the African continent. On the case of natural resource management and environmental conservation in less developed countries, for example, the theme of sustainable natural resource use through local community participation and indigenous conservation epistemologies has been on the international agenda since the first global environmental conference in Stockholm, Sweden in 1972. In this conference, resource depletion, the continued damage of the ozone layer, and environment degradation such as increasing desertification, soil erosion, and declining biodiversity in terrestrial and aquatic resources were all attributed to the exclusion of local communities in resource management and state centred approach to common pool resource management[1] or common property. Such deliberations though were raised in view of natural resources and the environment came as a shocking challenge to Western science that for centuries now had enjoyed the sole task of dealing with all issues that affect humans and their environment. In continents such as Africa, where non-Western epistemologies had suffered relegation since the advent of colonialism, the 1972 Stockholm conference deliberations were understood as a clarion call for the restoration of other epistemologies – what is commonly referred to as IKSs – to complement Western knowledge in resolving problems that affect humanity.

Yet, with the 'high' waves of globalisation, the restoration and reinstitution of other knowledge forms to complement Western knowledge has always been too slow or rather insignificant in societies such as those of Africa. This has been largely because while globalisation was meant to facilitate the movement of goods, communication and people in the world – a global village – in reality the movement has been one sided. There has been asymmetrical relations between societies, particularly between those that are duped 'developed nations' such as Europe and America and the so-called developing nations such as Africa, in terms of the movement of ideas, cultural values and goods. Developed nations, especially Europe and America, have in fact represented the world such that all that is Euro-American is what has been considered global while all that is non-Euro-American has been considered local. This means that in this globalisation deal, there are some societies (such as Europe and America) that consider themselves as more equal than others. A fair deal would be that all societies (whether considered as developed or developing) should participate equally in the globalisation of cultural values, goods and ideas. Otherwise, what should be understood as 'globalisation' would be, at best, replacement of cultural, socio-economic and political values of the societies that are considered developing by those of the societies that are considered as developed. This would, therefore, be another form of imperialism perpetrated in the name of globalisation. And given that societies like Africa have already suffered imperialism in the false name of civilisation during colonialism, it will be a damning thing by scholars and theorists of the present day to allow such a thing happening without giving a signal to the 'common people'.

While many scholars have looked at the problems associated with the impact of globalisation on Africa since the pre-colonial era through the present time, they have done this largely in form of paper presentations and publication. Besides, most scholars have avoided providing comprehensive texts and theorisation about the possible future of the African continent in view of her experiences, past and present. To date, there are very few books that have been produced especially by African scholars (on the continent or in the diasporan communities) theorising the future of Africa or tackling the issue of globalisation, particularly rethinking its impacts on the so-called developing societies such as Africa. This makes the present book a critical text that lays the foundation for re-theorising globalisation as a controversial complex process especially from an African perspective; a book that provides a firm foundation to counterbalance the continued Western socio-economic and political dominance and arrogance as well as increasing the socio-economic and political space of Africa and its developing world allies alike. Besides, the book departs from standard treatments in world studies by attempting to demystify the long standing myths and dangerous assumption by many Euro-American scholars that globalisation is doing more good than harm. This should not be translated to mean – and cannot be rightly interpreted to mean – that positives associated with globalisation are not acknowledged in this book. What is emphasised in this book, however, is the argument that in many African societies the negatives associated with globalisation seem to outweigh the positives. Unfortunately, the assumption of an all-encompassing globalisation has come to dominate both scholarly and political analysis to the point that anyone who might make an attempt to contest it runs the risk of being automatically treated with contempt. Yet truly speaking, a critical question that boggles the minds of many critical thinkers especially from Africa or elsewhere when it comes to globalisation in Africa is: "What does it really mean to be global?" or more specifically "Are Europe and America the global?"

I should be quick to point out that I have committed myself and garnered extra-ordinary courage to do a project such as this for the major reason of the love of faithful scholarship and prevalence of 'true' justice in Africa and the world-over. I have, thus, committed myself to challenge continued Euro-American imperialism on Africa that seem to be blind to the consequences of its own *politics* by explicitly arguing that most of the problems – political, social, environmental, moral etc. – of the African continent are intimately bound up with the history of European settlement on the African soils and the social inequalities they caused thereafter (see also Mawere 2014). As such, in order to undertake a critical analysis of the African problems and deal with them accordingly, we must know their generic and historical roots.

While I cannot prophesy that this book will answer all questions about the envisaged future of Africa and in particular the impact of processes such as globalisation in post-colonial Africa as well as the renewed relationship between China and Africa, I remain fervently hopeful that the facts and critical interpretation that follow will make a significant contribution towards the reinforcement of my major argument that globalisation has a double impact on people's societies: it has benefitted some societies while impoverishing others in ways too numerous to mention. Yet in the ideal sense of globalisation, norms, values, knowledge practices, goods and services should be mutually shared without one society dominating the other(s). A number of suggestions on how the present scenario around issues concerned with globalisation are provided in many of the chapters that run throughout this book. The book is a valuable asset for policy makers, institutional planners, conservation sciences, practitioners and students of world studies, social/cultural anthropology, education, development studies, African studies, heritage studies, and political/social ecology.

Chapter 1

African cultures and globalisation: The impact of globalisation on the posterity of African cultures with reference to Mozambique, South Africa and Zimbabwe

Introduction

Africa has a heterogeneous society that offers many opportunities for cross-cultural research. Whilst authors on culture and mass media generally agree that people are identified by their cultures and that mass media affect culture in one way or another, there is patchy literature by [indigenous] Africans and Mozambican, South African and Zimbabwean authors in particular, on the impact of mass media on African cultures. In the light of this observation, it is apparent that there is the need for comprehensive research on Africa in this twilight zone especially in the aforementioned countries where the mantra of Western [mass] media (heretofore referred to as mass media) is having a dramatic effect on culture. Though also making reference to South Africa, Mozambique and Zimbabwe, this chapter will make special reference and draw more examples (or case studies) from Mozambique for the mere reason that it is one country in the southern African region where dramatic cultural transformations are taking a centre stage. As such, Mozambique represents many other countries in the region where similar transformations are being experienced. The drawing of examples from three countries in southern Africa while making special reference to one country (Mozambique) is done to hone the issue of focus, to avoid generalisations, and to justify the title of the book as a text that deals with cultural heritage in Africa.

1

Mozambican [traditional] culture, as with South African and Zimbabwean cultures, is communal rather than individualistic; traditionally, it is focused on relationships rather than being task oriented like the European culture. When asking for directions or upon meeting someone, it is polite to first greet the person and ask how they are doing and then go about business. Personal boundaries are practically non-existent as is evident, for example, in the South African adage: '*muntu muntu ngabantu*/a person is a person because of others' (Shutte 2001) or the African aphorism 'I am because we are, we are therefore I am' (Mbiti 1999: 145). However, due to mass media that is fast spreading its tentacles across the southern African region through the tide of globalisation that has swept across the African continent, acculturation is fast gaining ground. This means that like many other Southern African cultures, Mozambican culture is facing a new set of challenges, coupled with classic hindrances as it joins the global community. One of these challenges is the uncertain trajectory of mass media, particularly television, which has both positive and negative impacts on culture.

The impact of mass media on Mozambican culture however varies from province to province or generally from place to place. Whilst culture and traditional ways of life are still well preserved from the central to the northern provinces of the country, the opposite is true in the southern provinces and in towns and cities. The Makonde people, from Cabo Delgado Province in the north-east, for example, are known for their traditional fearlessness and initiation rituals. They are also accomplished craftsmen, producing fine hardwood mainly mahogany, ebony or ironwood-and ivory carvings which often depict the stories of earlier generations. Music is also part of the Mozambican culture and is very important to the Niassa people who live in the sparsely populated north-western region. The agility of the Nhau dancers of Tete Province is much admired. To the sound of resounding drum beats, they dance holding huge and frightening wooden masks. For the Chopi people of Inhambane Province (in the Central), the 'timbila' is both the name of a local xylophone and a wonderful dance. They also play 'mbira', made of strips of metal attached to a hollow box and plucked with the fingers. Besides, visual art is also important in the Mozambican culture. The Macua women, from Nampula Province are known for their art and craftsmanship. They paint their faces with 'muciro', a white, root extract. They also make straw baskets, mats and sculptures from ebony and clay. The traditional, spicy cooking of Zambezia is highly regarded. Zambezia chicken, grilled with palm oil, is a particular delicacy. All this is a testimony that the traditional culture of Mozambique as is still preserved in central and northern regions is rich and admirable.

Nevertheless, mass media and acculturation have resulted in most of the elements of the Mozambican culture and traditional ways of life fast disappearing from the scene. In towns and cities as with the southern provinces, the impact of mass media and cultural diffusion is more visible than in the countryside and other provinces. This chapter examines the impact of mass media, especially television, on the Mozambican, South African and Zimbabwean (hereafter African) cultures. More importantly, the chapter argues that though mass media has some positive impact on development, it has to be used with care and caution. This argument is borne from the observation that the impact of mass media on any culture is critical and will substantively affect the future in ways too numerous to mention. In this light, the chapter philosophises that in the face of mass media, the future of Mozambican culture will only reside in its ability to address a number of theoretical, political and socio-cultural questions which confront the present and the next generation. Put differently, for African cultures to flourish the issue of mass media must be discussed, addressed and mitigated against. Otherwise, African cultures are threatened and consequently face a 'slow death' such that one day they might disappear the dinosaurs' way if no instantaneous action is taken.

Conceptual clarifications: Culture, mass media and globalisation

The terms culture and mass media do not always mean the same thing to everybody. For reasons of clarity and precision, it is prudent that the terms are discussed separately.

Culture

Culture derives from the Latin word *cultura* stemming from *colere* meaning 'to cultivate' (Bastian, 2009). However, the concept and definition of culture have been well documented in the literature, and scholars have provided a number of interpretations to the term: in fact, culture is a contested term, with widely varying definitions and interpretations. The term culture, thus, has proven to be elusive and complex perhaps chiefly due to its wider scope and nature. The complexity of coming up with a universally agreed definition of culture is predicted by the fact that social problems differ from society to society and this tend to define the role that culture has to play in society as well as the expectations of society on how and to what extent culture should help solving economic and socio-political problems. Yet the absence of a specific and widely agreed definition makes culture vulnerable to confliction interpretation by scholars. This has led Alfred Kroeber and Clyde Kluckhohn (1952) to compile a list of 164 definitions of culture. Since then, several authors have formulated a broad definition for culture describing it with different terms such as basic assumptions, feelings, values, behaviour, and so forth (Benedict, 1959; Sapir, 1991; Hall, 1992; Schein, 1992; Trampenaars, 1994; Giddens 1993). Benedict (1959), for instance, defines culture as the canons of choice. Kluckhohn and Strodbeck (1961) introduce the concept of value

4

orientations to explain the phenomenon of culture. Sapir (1977) suggests that culture is a silent language because different cultures present dissimilar perceptions about time, space, ownership, friendship and agreements. And, for Schein (1992:97), culture is a pattern of shared assumptions that a group of people learned as it solved its problems of external adaptation and internal integration that has worked well enough to be considered valid and, therefore, to be taught to new members as the correct way to perceive, think and fell in relation to those problems. Trompenaars (1994) proposes that culture directs people's actions. He observes that culture is man-made, confirmed by others, conventionalised and passed on for younger people or new comers to learn (ibid). This connotes that for Trompenaars culture provides people with a meaningful context in which to meet, to think about themselves and to face the outer world. Van der Walt holds almost a similar understanding of culture. For him (1997:8), 'culture is not only something alive': it is rich and complex as it includes habits, customs and social organisation, technology, language, norms, values, beliefs and much more. Trompenaars' definition of cultures is more or less the same as that given by Anthony Giddens. For Giddens (1993: 31), culture refers to 'the ways of life of the members of a society, or groups within a society'. This means that cultures includes many things and activities that members of a society or groups within a society engage themselves in such as religious ceremonies, their dressing codes and styles, marriage customs, leisure pursuits, kinships patterns, behavioural patterns, feeding habits and so on.

Though the concept of culture has been interpreted differently throughout history, as has been shown in this study, what cuts across a number of definitions that scholars have provided on the concept is the general belief that the concept is most commonly used in three basic senses I elaborate below:

♦ As an integrated pattern of human knowledge, belief and behaviour that depends upon the capacity for symbolic thought and social learning: culture in all societies, thus, is learned (or even unlearned) through observation and deliberate instruction. Culture is, however, not learned through natural inheritance.

♦ As the shared attitudes, values, goals and practices that characterises an institution, organisation or group that are dynamic. This connotes that culture is never static as interaction between people within one society and between societies always exist. Under normal circumstances, continual change of culture is, however, not abrupt but slow – indeed very slow except where coercion is involved.

♦ As excellence of taste in the fine arts and humanities, also known as high culture.

As previously highlighted the precise definition of culture is in fact elusive. The three basic senses seem to be captured in different definitions of culture discussed in the preceding paragraphs. In view of the three senses and for purposes of this work, culture shall be understood as an integrated pattern of human knowledge, beliefs, behaviour, values, attitudes, goals and practices that characterises an institution, organisation or group of people. A similar understanding is aptly captured by Toyin Falola (2003: 1, emphasis mine) when he says 'the definition and meaning of culture are broad: values, beliefs, texts about the beliefs and ideas, multiple daily practices, aesthetic forms, systems of communication (e.g. language), institutions of society, a variety of experiences that capture *a people's* way of life, [...] political ideas, *and* ideology'. The fundamental idea of culture thus is that it reflects both the social imperatives and the social consequences of human behaviour (in a given society) in their conduct with others.

Mass media

Until recently, mass media was clearly defined as any medium used to transmit mass communication comprising the eight mass media industries; books, newspapers, magazines, recordings, radio, movies, television and the Internet (Lane 2007). It has been understood as the transmission and reception of 'messages' on a very large scale. However, the term mass media has become a multivalent term: it is no longer easy to define due to constant creation of new digital communication technology that is now in abundance. Historically, the term mass media was coined in the 1920s with the advent of nationwide radio networks, mass-circulation newspapers and magazines (Bastian, 2009). It should be noted however that some forms of mass media such as drama, books and manuscripts had already been in the use centuries before. The term denotes 'a section of the media specifically designed to reach a very large audience such as the population of a nation state' (ibid). This now includes mobile phones and the eight media industries mentioned above.

The term 'public media' has a similar meaning: 'it is the sum of the public mass distributors of news and entertainment across media such as newspapers, television, radio and broadcasting' (ibid). The purposes of mass media include advocacy (advertising, marketing, propaganda, public relation and political communication), entertainment (music, acting, sports, reading, video, computer games) and public service announcements. There are a rich theoretical discussions on the subject of mass media, and I will not engage this voluminous literature; instead, I will illuminate the benefits and challenges posed by television media vis-à-vis the current and future of Mozambican culture. Thus for purposes of this work, the term mass media shall be used to refer to television mass media industry. This is because the impact of television on Mozambican culture is greater than any other mass media industry existing in the country so far.

7

Globalisation

Mass media is one example through which globalisation as a process is manifesting itself. Given that the concept of globalisation is highly controversial, its impact and that of the society have been understood differently in different societies: globalisation as a process has yielded divergent views from different scholars across the world especially on the nature and impact of the process on different societies. By globalisation, I mean the process of international interactions of all kind whereby nations share cultures, goods, capitals, services, information, and so on amongst themselves: it is an integration process of different consenting societies into a common system for the enhancement of a global world. I should underline that this is my understanding of globalisation as a process that is neutral and with mutual cultural gains amongst societies – a process that ideally should be culturally and consciously (or unconsciously) controlled by all societies in the world and ought to equally benefit all societies by taking something of the other but without depriving others. As a process on its own, globalisation started a long time ago given that societies all over the world have always been interacting with each other though in varying degrees and circumstances. With Europe and America, contacts with Africa, for example, were established as early as the 15th Century. And within African societies themselves, contacts with each other have always been existent since the beginning of history in Africa. Globalisation has, however, been popularised during and after the trans-Atlantic racial slave trade as well as the colonisation process of nations in the world by Western imperial countries and subsequently America. But does globalisation really brings the enhancement of the global world? Or who benefits and who loses in this whole game? These questions and many others that examine whether globalisation is a neutral process, a process that brings only positive or negative results or both positive and negative results, continue to boggle the minds of many especially when considering globalisation vis-a-vis Africa. In Africa, the problem that many scholars have noted in view of globalisation is the tendency of some countries in the West to swallow-up and dominate other people's cultures – emphasising the need to embrace Western norms and values –, a common trend that can be traced from the [racial] slave period through the present time. This has been described as 'forced acculturation'(Ekwuru 1999) or cultural atrophy of the so-called Third World Countries by those of the so-called Developed Countries in the name of globalisation as Western ways of life are being adopted (willingly or through force) by societies in the Third World as the normal way of life. It is also in view of observations such as this that some scholars have understood globalisation only in negative terms: substantial criticism, thus, has been directed towards globalisation. Geller (1995), for instance, has described globalisation as a system of political, economic, and cultural domination forcibly imposed by a technologically advanced foreign minority on an indigenous majority. Likewise, Aborishade (2002) understands globalisation as Western imperialism, particularly American imperialism that seeks to impose its hegemony on other subjugated and exploited nations' threat of economic, political or military coercion. For him, globalisation is criticised for widening the gap between the so-called rich and periphery nations as it seeks to wage unprecedented attacks on the welfare and rights of poor nations. In fact it is common knowledge that where different cultures come into contact, the one with a highly developed media technology and other such expression techniques tend to develop a domineering posture over the other cultures (the weaker cultures) as the latter are normally lured to borrow extensively from the former. Unfortunately, this is the current situation that Africa is facing. Globalisation understood this way and in the context of Africa is what one may describe as the cultural rape of the African continent by the Western imperial countries – a process that has always had negative cultural, political, religious and economic impact on the African societies. Yet the nature and degree at which globalisation impact on different cultures remains a complex question to understand and unpack due to the complexities around global politics. Though plausible for some positives, it is also this negative precept associated with globalisation in Africa that has led many critical scholars to view it as an ambiguous or paradoxical process.

Background to the Mozambican culture

Mozambican culture is one of the oldest cultures in Africa yet it is so diverse as to be impossible to pin down and define. This is because the South, Central and the Northern regions have their own distinct cultures and every ethnic group has carved its own cultural niche. However, there are some cultural elements that were traditionally respected and valued across all dialectical groups in the country (Mawere, 2010). These elements together with the shared history of colonisation and the following struggle for independence from the Portuguese are a common thread that bound Mozambicans as a people with a common identity. Even today, culture and its preservation matters a great deal to Mozambicans, at least in rhetoric. The government of Mozambique with the initiative of UNESCO has even formulated a 'Cultural Policy' which lays as its objectives protection and preservation of cultural heritage of the country, inculcating Mozambican art consciousness amongst Mozambicans and promoting high standards in creative and performing arts.

Unfortunately, the advent of mass media has made the cultural policy largely redundant as traditional forms of arts seem to have virtually disappeared or rather slipped on the verge of slow death. This is because mass media has the power to change people's world views. Benjamin Page (1996: 23) agrees to this when he observes that 'a large body of evidence now indicated that what appears in print or on the air has a

10

substantial impact upon how citizens think and what they think about: e.g., what they cite as important problems' or important things to do. Ramsden (1996) also argues that mass media has the ability to influence people's attitude and behaviour. Traditionally, Mozambican culture is not only limited to material manifestations such as monuments and objects that were preserved over time. It also includes living expressions and the traditions; intangible heritage that Mozambican communities have inherited from their ancestors and transmit to their descendants, in most cases orally.

In terms of tangible heritage, clothing is one important aspect of the Mozambican culture. Traditionally, the Mozambican women are decently dressed in long clothes that hide knees inside. Married women normally cover their hair and wore wrapping clothes on top of the long dress. Likewise, men are dressed in long trousers and shirts which cover almost all body parts. Visual art is another key aspect of the Mozambican culture. The Macua women, from the north-eastern Nampula Province are known for their art and craftsmanship in straw baskets, mats and sculptures from ebony and clay. The traditional, spicy cooking of Zambezia is highly regarded. Zambezia chicken, grilled with palm oil, is a particular delicacy. The Island of Mozambique and Mozambique museum are other significant tangible cultural features of the country.

Mozambique also traditionally regards its intangible heritage as a matter of active concern. The Chopi's *Timbila*, a traditional musical expression, for example, was declared a masterpiece of the Oral and Intangible Heritage of humanity in Mozambique in 2005 (UNESCO Report, 2005). The *Makonde*, from Cabo Delgado Province in the north-east, for example, are known for their fearlessness and initiation rituals. The *Makonde* are also accomplished craftsmen, producing fine hardwood mainly mahogany, ebony or ironwood and ivory carvings which often depict the stories of earlier generations.

Music is also part of the Mozambican culture and is very important to the Niassa people who live in the sparsely populated north-western region. The agility of the *Nhau* dancers of Tete Province is much admired. To the sound of resounding drum beats, they dance holding huge and frightening wooden masks.

The other important aspect of Mozambican culture is language. As given by the German romanticists of the 19th century such as Herder, Wondt and Humbolt, language is not just acting as one cultural trait among many but rather as the direct expression of a people's national character and as such as culture in a kind of condensed form. Herder (1744-1803), for example, suggests, 'since every people is a People, it has its own national culture expressed through its own language'. In the same line of thought, Franz Boas (1920) argues 'the fact that intellectual culture of a people is largely constructed, shared and maintained through the use of language means it is unimaginable to study the culture of a foreign people without also becoming acquainted with their language'. In Mozambique, the official language is Portuguese but each ethnic group has its own vernacular language that defines it as a group. Another important part of the Mozambican culture is its focus on relationships rather than being task oriented like the European culture. When asking for directions or upon meeting someone, it is polite to first greet the person and ask how they are doing and then go about business. Personal boundaries are practically non-existent. In fact, the traditional life of Mozambicans is communal rather than individualistic.

Globalisation and mass media: Impacts on the Mozambican culture

It is beyond question that media plays many different and possibly incompatible roles (Mawere, 2012). For the audiences, it is a source of entertainment and information while for media workers, media is an industry that offers jobs and therefore income, prestige and professional identity. For the owners, media is not only a source of profit but a source of power. For society at large, the media can be a way to transmit information and values. Thus, depending on whose perspective and which role we focus on, we might see a different picture of mass media. Likewise, the impact of mass media depends on whose perspective and on the role we focus. And for this reason, mass media in many societies has invited and incited serious debates as it can be viewed from both positive and negative perspectives. As such, mass media has impacted the Mozambican culture in ways too numerous to mention. On one hand, it has brought many positive changes in the Mozambican culture. And on the other hand, a number of negative impacts can be pointed out especially from African traditionalist and moralistic viewpoints.

The advent of mass media has influenced a number of changes in Mozambican traditions, customs and values. Although it is a well-known fact that culture is dynamic and never static, the impact of mass media on Mozambican culture is so tremendous that it becomes imperative for the issue to be discussed, addressed and mitigated against before it is too late. It is worth noting, however, that the impact of mass media on Mozambican culture varies from one area to another. In the southern provinces of the country, cities and towns, for example, mass media has had more impact – both positive and negative – than in the countryside. The ensuing paragraphs discuss how mass media has impacted the Mozambican culture.

The positive impact of mass media on the Mozambican culture

The advent of mass media in Mozambique, as in any other society in the world has brought about a number of positive changes. As means of communication, mass media is playing

13

an important role in Mozambique. Unlike in the old days when messages took months to reach their destined audiences, through mass media such as TVs, they are now fast reaching the designated recipients/masses in all corners of the country. In the war against HIV/AIDS, for example, mass media is helping a great deal in sending the message to the public to change the risky sexual behaviour and promote awareness of the pandemic in youth and the public in general. Agha (2003) confirms that the exposure to mass media messages concerning HIV/AIDS reduces personal risks and promotes condom use as an attractive lifestyle choice thereby contributing to development of perceptions that are conducive to the adoption of condom use and HIV/AIDS prevention.

With Mozambique's low literacy rate, mass media has also become a powerful socialising agent (Graber, 1980) and a facilitator in knowledge pollination. School subjects such as English, Geography, and Mathematics are learnt on television. With the same objective, mass media generates interesting debates on socio-economic and political issues. The STV and *Mira Mar* channels, for example, sometimes discuss political issues to do with justice, human rights and democracy. This is positive as politicians and academics rely heavily on media to communicate their messages. In more or less the same way, the general members of the public are affected by mass media on how they learn about their world and interact with others inside and outside the world of politics. In Mozambique, media thus is helping in transmitting knowledge, sensitising people of their rights and in reducing the illiteracy rate which is currently 43% (Ali, 2009).Thus mass media has a significant role in disseminating knowledge and in promoting academic excellence.

Besides, it is now a reality that in Mozambique mass media otherwise seconded by soccer has become a leading entertainer for most families. During spare time, people can entertain themselves watching sports, films and other entertaining programmes such as soap opera (*Novela*) like *Poderes Paralelos* (Parallel powers), *show de talent* (Talent show), among others that are often shown on Mozambican channels. However, not all that mass media brings to the Mozambicans is beneficial when considering its culture. In fact, it seems more harm than good is being done to the Mozambican culture through mass media. The next section of this chapter, therefore, examines the negative impact of mass media on the Mozambican culture.

Media imperialism and the African cultures: A closer look at the negative impact of mass media on the Mozambican culture

There is a visible negative impact of mass media on the personality development of adolescents (Puri, 2006) in most if not all cultures. Mass media is largely a product of the Western world that the latter has either imposed on non-Western societies or lured non-Western societies to adopt through unscrupulous advertisements and other such sophisticated technological expressions. What is most worrying about the impact of mass media particularly on the African societies (e.g. Mozambique) is that it is causing the African people to lose that which define them as a people. Now that any culture is societally based, the destruction of a culture entails the destruction of the society, which the culture in question defines. In the context of Africa vis-a-vis Western cultures, this means the cultural atrophy of the African societies. This is in turn generating a cultural identity crisis on the continent. Consequently, concern from parents, professionals and the populace at large about the impact of mass media on children and adolescents has grown steadily over recent years as the tide of globalisation continues sweeping across the continent. It is, therefore, imperative to examine and understand the role of media exposure on children and adolescents in African in general and Mozambique in particular in order to diagnose and

15

treat behavioural problems as well as to prevent further tragedies and disorders on culture and in the personality of the adolescents.

For some Mozambicans, mass media has resulted in 'forced acculturation' (Ekwuru 1999). Forced acculturation is a process whereby individuals or groups of people in one society are forced to receive and adopt norms and values of another (outside) society normally by the outsiders who perceive themselves to be more superior. A case in point is the coercion that was perpetrated by Western imperial countries on African countries during colonialism when they [Western imperialists] imposed their own knowledge, practices, cultural norms and values on Africans.

Mass media is one 'technological device' that has always been and continues to be capitulated to ensure that cultural values are transmitted from one society to another. For this reason, mass media does assimilation, and though advancing into new technology may seem very exciting and futuristic, this may not necessarily be a good thing. This is chiefly because with mass communication devices people are sending the 'wrong message' to different cultures and especially the youth. In Mozambique, music, drama and literature have all changed with time due to the advent of mass media communication system. In towns, cities and generally the southern provinces, the impact is even on the rise due to the increase of foreign channels owners who are capitalising on the channel. Mozambique being one of the poorest countries in the world, its economy is controlled by the rich Western countries. So are some of its television channels. The channels are dominated by the Portuguese (R.T.P Africa) and the Brazilian (*Mira Mar*) television channels. The Brazilian Universal Church sponsored television channel, *Mira Mar* has too much sex and talk shows which stretch too far if we are to consider the Mozambican culture where the channel exists. In fact, it presents a plethora of programmes with sexual overtones. *Vai dar namoro*, literally mean (Go and make love), *Gugu* and *Tudo é possivel* (Everything is possible) are cases in point. So is the STV programme called '*Music box*'. These programmes present naked (both men and women with only painted bodies) and semi-naked people (with bras and pants only) especially women dancing and sometimes making love – fondling each other or sleeping together – in the public amphitheatre. This is a taboo in the Mozambican culture and by extension the African traditional culture. Such cultural atrophy has resulted in the erosion of traditional norms and values and consequently the decline of non-Western traditional cultures as those of Africa all in the name of globalisation.

It is even surprising to hear that the channel is sponsored by a church – the Brazilian Universal Church of God – given its contents. From an African traditional view, such programmes are irritating especially when watching with one's in-laws, daughters or mothers, among other family members. The dangers are not just in the content, but more importantly, in volume. If one sees something once, he [she] can dismiss it as aberrant; if sees it continuously, however, at some point, one is left with a sense of being out of step with mainstream beliefs and values (Frick, 2008). The sexual overtones that the channel frequently presents have resulted in many interpreting it as a promoter of prostitution and cultural decadence amongst the Mozambican youths. Many young people are no longer dressing in a 'decent African way' imitating the way actors in these channels dress. They have become perpetual zombies of the West. It is now a common thing to see young girls walking around the city with just small tight skirts (mini-skirts) or with tight small shorts akin to waist belts. Young people can now make love in the open, even in the road; a thing that was unheard of or rather 'a taboo' in the past in Mozambique. They now think that culture is the 'Western culture' forgetting their own 'roots'. In cities and towns, it is no longer a taboo to see people of opposite sexes urinating side by side in the public where pedestrians are passing by. The law doesn't even prohibit this although in some other African countries like South Africa and Zimbabwe, such people would be charged with public indecency and are, therefore, liable to fine or even a jail term. This is because sexual organs are offensive in the African traditional culture and should not be exposed in the public. The change of behaviour and attitude by Mozambicans especially the young people is, therefore, negative and worrying not only to the Mozambican culture, but to the African culture as a whole. This change of behaviour and attitude has invoked traditionalists and moralists in the country to argue for the banning of the programmes or rather the channels themselves even though this might raise a number of questions from an economic perspective. Economically, Mozambique depends largely on Brazil and Portugal besides China.

In addition, other Mozambican traditional social structures, customs and values are fast disappearing from the scene. Communication which often took a wonderful musical tone especially in the communication of literature, political and socio-economic works is dying away. The religious and epistemological roles of the traditional folktales have been down-played while their didactic and moral aspects have been, however, overtaken by mass media. Folktales were passed down generations verbally by a storyteller who usually was an old man or an old woman who has past child-bearing age. Mozambican traditional culture upholds these octogenarians as custodians of wisdom and knowledge. The advent of television, however, has made this rather obsolete. The traditions of village theatre and dance, folklore and story-telling thus are now history in the Mozambican culture. These were used as forms of entertainment and education (to impart good moral values that would prepare them for adult ritualistic society) in the youth. These traditions also offered a curriculum that prepared the children for their present and adult life, a curriculum that so far has been seconded and imitated by none. Thus due to mass media, folklore and story-telling have lost their following and thereby changing the traditional social structures of the Mozambican people. Instead of the youth gathering around a story teller who was an accredited and experienced old person in the community, they now gather around televisions watching films and other programmes. And since 'no child is born with a culture' (Barker 1994: 4), but learn that in which they are born into, young people are picking up the negative aspects presented by the above stated cultures to the next generation. Mozambique has a socially oriented culture (Bower 2007). It is focused on relationships rather than being task-oriented like the American culture (ibid). When asking for directions or upon meeting someone, for example, it is polite to first greet the person and ask how they are doing and then go about business. Life is communal rather than individualistic. If a child were to steal from a neighbour, it would be the neighbour's responsibility to spank the child rather than the parent. Likewise, if one were to yell, 'thief!' in a market, the crowd would gang up and beat the thief. All this is because justice is carried out communally in the traditional Mozambican culture. However, since the advent of mass media all these social and communal values of the Mozambican culture are fast loosing favour to the individualistic western values. Many Mozambicans are now cultivating the materialistic and individualistic habits that prior to the advent of globalisation in the form of colonialism and latter mass media were values associated with the Western culture. This is not only happening in Mozambique alone, but in many other African societies. Concerned with the same problem, UwaezuokeObioha (2008) observed of the Igbo people of Nigeria that the culture of individualism is fast eroding the values and ideals of the extended family system which Nigerians especially the Igbo are well known for. Back to the case study for this chapter, Mozambique, the Brazilian *Mira Mar* channel has many programmes such as operas *(for example, poderes paralelos)* which emphasise that one's life is a private business and no one should bother another person's life. Today, if one yells, 'thief!' in *Chipamanine* market in Maputo, no one would even turn eyes to the thief. If a child steals from a neighbour and the neighbour disciplines the child, beware! The next day the neighbour would receive *summons* from police. This is all because of 'split-personality crisis' (Mawere 2011: 1) and excessive individualism that is setting roots and fast eroding the traditional norms and values of the Mozambican people.

Also, it is now a common thing in Mozambique that people enter into business without formally greeting one another first, – which is alien to the African culture. In fact, entering into business before formal greetings is considered inhumane and morally wrong in the African traditional culture.

It can also be noted that the content of music by Mozambican musicians, as with many other musicians across Africa, has changed significantly due to mass media with most of the musicians concentrating much on beat/rhythm and not on message. Some of the songs famous in the music fraternity today are full of sexual overtones and innuendos. Manuel Mazoi's (whose trade name is Oliver Style) *Tira ropa* (put off your clothes) and Mr Roger and Ziqo's Dog Style are good examples. The former song, sung in Portuguese and Changani, and whose genre is known as *Marabenta* is sung as:

Vocal: Tira ropa (x4) (Put off your clothes)
Chorus: Tira! (x4) (Put off!)
Vocal: Timila xifambo (Put off your shoes)
Chorus: Timila! (Put off!)
Vocal: Timila buluku (Put off your trouser/short)
Chorus: Timila! (Put off!)
Vocal: Tsalingeni kei? (x4) (What about the underwear?)
Chorus: Timila! (x4) (Put off!).

In Zimbabwe, songs such as Jacob Moyana's *Kana munotidako tichauyako* (literally translated as *if you say big buttocks everywhere then we shall come there*) has been criticised for its ambiguity and contents that are seen by many as obscene and morally insulting. The controversial song that is considered by many as full of sexually suggestive language is sung as:

KuChipinge munotidako (If you say big buttocks in Chipinge)
KwaMutare munotidako (If you say big buttocks in Mutare)
KuChiredzi munotidako (If you say big buttocks in Chiredzi)
KuBeitbridge (If you say big buttocks in Beitbridge)
Tagara munotidako; makatichaira foni kuti munotidako; tichatogara tichiuyako kana muchitidako (If you say big buttocks everywhere then we shall come there).

While the song could also be possibly interpreted as meaning that if you want us everywhere (i.e. Chipinge, Mutare, Chiredzi and Beitbridge) then we shall always come there, the first meaning seems to be more pervasive among listeners. In fact, the first interpretation makes the song unpalatable and morally insulting, hence unsuitable for public consumption. While the artist, Moyana, could possibly defend himself as being stressing the second meaning of the song, the fact that the song has since its release never received airplay on any of the nation's radio stations and that the viral version of the song has a woman with huge buttocks suggestively playing to it makes it clear that the first interpretation is considered by many people in the country. I argue in this chapter that artists have the same responsibility as that of the parents, pastors, teachers and novelists. They should be morally responsible given that they are role models of the society especially for the young. What then would the society think of an artist who lead the youths astray or of the teacher who teaches bad content? It is, therefore, after critical analysis of the contents of the aforementioned song that I surmise that they are morally unacceptable in many African societies such as Zimbabwe. So are the contents of the first song by the Mozambican musician, Mazoi.

The content of Mazoi's song has been argued by moralists and traditionalists alike to be promoting prostitution, immorality and social disharmony in the traditional Mozambican culture. In many occasions, it has been reported that in some public drinking occasions like beer parties people dance this song putting off their clothes one by one as the song commands until they are naked. The content of this song is greatly influenced by loss of direction on the cultural values by the artists. Because of what they normally see happening on television, it is no longer a taboo for them to talk about putting off clothes in the public. With similar sexual innuendos is DJ Aridilas' *Ainda por cima voĉe jinca* (even in bed on top of me you still complain). As is the case of Oliver Style's *Tira ropa*, one can read the immoral tone of Aridilas' song right from its title.

Some controversial programmes offered by the *Mira Mar* television channel are the *Show international blue man* and *Jogos com as Circo Pindora maos menores artistas do Brazil*. In these two programmes, one person is asked to stand still in front of a data board with legs apart. Another person stands on the opposite side with five extremely sharp knives. He will then start throwing the knives fiercely one by one, one just on top of the head of the person in front. The other two are thrown on sides at waist height. The forth one is thrown exactly between the legs and the last one on either side of the leg but at knee height. The person in front should be courageous enough not to move an inch. Otherwise, he [she] will be finished. The game is not only frightening but life risking. It shows images of violence and aggression. If one of the knives is misdirected and get into the flesh of that in front he [she] is dead. In the Mozambican traditional culture, such games are considered devilish and unacceptable. Besides, children may imitate such games. Given the natural experimenting habit of children and that the game requires a high degree of expertise, these games can be argued to promote social delinquencies that may result in loss of lives or fatal injuries among children.

In Mozambique as elsewhere in Africa, such immoral acts are not only gaining roots in music but also in legal milieu. In South Africa, for example, a top court recently (in October 2013) declared it legal for children as young as 12 years old to engage themselves in sexual activities with other children. As reported by Mfundekelwa Mkhulisi in the Daily sun of South Africa (4/10/2013):

> South Africa's top court made it legal for children as young as 12 to have sex. The ruling means teenagers between the ages of 12 and 16 need no longer fear legal consequences if they engage in sexual activity. The Constitutional Court said, 'in effect, children of that age were having sex anyway'. It declared sections 15 and 16 of the Sexual Offences Act, which criminalised kissing, petting and penetration between young teenagers, to be unconstitutional (pp. 1).

I argue in this chapter that such a ruling is equal to licensing immorality in the African societies (and in particular South Africa) in the name of the global talk on children's human rights. Besides, it is 'un-African' considering that in Africa, in general, sexual activities are considered a taboo and also not for children. I add that even the reason for the ruling that "in effect, children of that age were having sex anyway" doesn't hold water. It is as good as legalising robbery and murder on the pretext that though illegal people still commit those crimes. Such a ruling, therefore, does not only defy the logic of morality and reason, but also a call for poverty among young Africans as these are likely to destroy their aspirations and hope for good life early in life, that is, as soon as they engage in sexual activities and contract diseases or get pregnant.

Another critical issue that mass media is seriously aggravating is that of names. I understand a name as a tag or label for a noun (anything), normally used to distinguish one thing from the other. Names can identify a class or category of things, or a single thing, either uniquely, or within a given context. A personal name identifies a specific unique and identifiable individual person, but in 'a given context'. As such, Mozambican names identify Mozambicans in their context from people of other contexts. However, this is appearing otherwise in Mozambique as traditional names been shunned since colonial period. Surprisingly, this seems to worsen even years after independence. Part of the reason for this is that the content in mass media is largely Western and names of participants (presenters, actors/artists) in these media channels are foreign, mainly Portuguese. Presented with such a scenario time and again in *novellas*– operas and other TV programmes, most children and even adults in Mozambique tend to do what Shakespeare portrays in his *What's in a name? That we call a rose*, where 'Romeo out of passion for Juliet, rejects his family name and vows, as Juliet asks, to 'deny (his) father' and instead be 'new baptised' as Juliet's lover' (eNotes-Shakespeare, 2010). Most Mozambicans thus have shunned their traditional names in favour of the Portuguese ones. As of now, one can hardly encounter a single Mozambican of the contemporary generation with a traditional name. Actually, if a child/person identifies himself/herself with a traditional name at school or anywhere else in the country he [she] will be laughed at or rather mocked. This hatred of one's own culture is grievous and shameful that it cannot go unchallenged especially in the African context where traditional names are literal and carry meaning to one's own life, family or society.

The same is true even in the Western tradition. Blake (2009) confirms that 'names can reveal much about your family history' since sources from which names are derived include nicknames, physical attributes, place of origin, trades, heraldic charges, and almost every object known to mankind that is related to the person in a way. Blake's conception identifies with Stallman who rightly notes that 'names convey meanings; our choice of names determines the meaning of what we say. An inappropriate name gives people the wrong idea' (Stallman 2009). For him and indeed so, a rose by any other name would smell as sweet – but if you call it a pen, people will be rather disappointed when they try to write with it. And if you call pens 'roses', people may not realise what they are good for. This serves to mean that 'names really matter for our communities because people who forget history are often condemned to repeat them' (ibid). In fact, the situations and problems that led Mozambicans develop traditional names are not completely eradicated, and they threaten to come back. It, therefore, remains paramount for Mozambicans to maintain their traditional names as they are 'custodians' and 'sources' of history to themselves and future generations. But to gain this revolutionary future, a better future different from the deplorable present, this must be a quick move towards cultural restoration – before foreign culture in Mozambique regains its composure and eliminates dissent and efforts as those demonstrated in this present work.

Recommendations

Media often acts as the bridge between our personal/private lives and the public world. We see ourselves and our place through mass media which bring to us news about some parts of the world where we happen to be absent. Given this nexus, there is need especially in Third World countries, to pay special attention to mass media lest we are manipulated by it. This is because Third World countries such as Mozambique are vulnerable to manipulation given that they lack the resources to maintain their own [cultural] independence. As argued by Reuss and Hiebert (1985) and indeed so, while mass media can be manipulated by the public, it is the former that normally manipulates the latter especially considering the state of affairs in many Third World countries where Western cultural products have become widely diffused and in many cases overtake the local ones. It is unfortunate that Africa has fallen victim of passive and thoughtless consumption of all Western norms and values even those that are traditionally Africans used to detest and frown at. In view of the dramatic effects of mass media in Mozambique, it is apparent that if nothing urgent is done to most of the programmes presented in the Mozambican channels, *media imperialism* or rather substantive cultural decadence would continue taking its toll.

I suggest that the Mozambican government [and of course all other African countries with similar situations] should set a separate ministry called 'Ministry of Culture and Communication'. This ministry would culturally sensor all programmes that have to do with culture before they are presented on television for public consumption. If a program is likely to cause discord on Mozambican culture then it would be replaced by that which deserves. The proposed ministry would also send its agents around the country gathering all information and promoting the Mozambican culture by presenting programmes with more local cultural content. It would be also imperative that the Ministry works hand in gloves with the Ministry of Education and Culture so that even in schools, emphasis on culture is more pronounced. Competitions on traditional dances, music, theatre and drama can be promoted right from school to national levels. This would catch the Mozambicans when they are still 'young' that they grow up conscious of their own culture. This would be a firm step to bring back the daunting Mozambican culture back on track. But to gain this revolutionary future, a better future

26

different from the deplorable present, this must be a quick move. Otherwise, Mozambican culture will soon be a history to its own people.

Concluding remarks

This chapter has argued that whilst it is acceptable that the Mozambican culture should progress together with the 'global village', Mozambicans should take a critical look at the role and impact of mass media and in particular external television programmes in their society. The following penetrating questions should be seriously considered before Mozambique 'grabs' on everything that foreign cultures bring through mass media:

♦Who owns the media?

♦Why are some images and ideas so prevalent in the mass media while others especially the local ones are marginalised?

♦Whose voices are represented and whose are not heard?

♦What impact do mass media have on culture? and,

♦How people use and interpret the mass media?

It is through critical analysis through these questions that Mozambique could realise how important it is to respect and preserve its own 'customs and traditional values' and ensure that these are carried on into the next generation. This analysis is critical because the mass media in Mozambique like elsewhere in Africa has, until today, systematically failed to act as the critical 'fourth state' that they pretended to be. Instead, mass media have consistently represented the interests of, and functioned as an integral component of the elites controlling society and determining policy and events. Yet it is the traditional values and customs shun by most television channels in the country that distinguish Mozambicans from people of other countries.

It is apparent that more harm than good is being done to the Mozambican culture. Besides dress, many other Mozambican cultural aspects have been sacrificed in favour of Western values brought to the Mozambican society mainly through mass media. The tradition of story-telling has taken a back seat in the Mozambican culture due to cassette playbacks of discourses. So is folk music. It has given way to cassettes and CDs. Drama and theatre arts have suffered the same consequences. They have diminished in importance under the stiff competition brought forth by mass media.

More importantly, it has been argued that due to mass media many traditional values in Mozambique and by extension Africa are now considered as 'outdated' and 'out of fashion' – that the aggressive spread of communication technologies have brought new obstructions and challenges to the African norms and values. Person to person interaction between strangers, for example, has nearly disappeared in towns and cities as information is now relayed through media channels: televisions, mobile phones, radios, books, newspapers and magazines. African identity thus is being given away to mass media yet in Africa a person is identified not only by 'rationality', but by culture. As such, Mozambique should preserve and safeguard its culture from decadence so as to ensure that its customs and values are passed on to the next generation undiluted. Programmes that mass media bring to Mozambican masses should be, therefore, culturally censored before they are presented for public consumption. This would at least ensure that the youth are not 'mentally corrupted' and made to unconsciously forget or despise their customs and values.

I should underscore my argument that although some programmes might be educative to audiences of high intellectual levels – the educated elites – the same programmes may yield opposite results when presented to uneducated masses and to people of a different culture. This is the case with the Brazilian Soap operas called *Novela– Poderes Paralelos* (parallel powers), *Tudo é posível* (everything is possible) that are presented on *STV* and *Mira Mar* channels that are widely watched across the country. In most cases, the message is understood and interpreted literally as it is presented due to the low literate level in Mozambique. And today, a lot of young women can afford walking around the city semi-naked or in very tight mini-skirts that expose the larger part of their bodies as they normally see in the operas. They are forgetting that in traditional Mozambique and by extension African traditional culture, thighs especially of a woman are offensive.

One of the major arguments that run throughout this chapter is that mass media is one of the goods and services dumped [by the Western countries] on Africa that are marketed by coercion and mass seductive advertisement which are blatantly superficial but nonetheless successful in creating desires in peoples of traditional societies (Akande 2002).In the light of this argument and the various observations noted in the preceding discussion, the chapter concludes that the issue of mass media is urgent and calls for profound and immediate action by the government and the public in general as the future of Mozambican culture, and by extension African cultures, will ultimately reside in the ability of the countries concerned to address a number of theoretical, political and socio-cultural questions which confront the present and the next generation. Otherwise, Mozambican culture would continually experience a 'slow death' and one day disappears the "dinosaurs' way" yet the need for knowledge, ideas and values from within [cultures] to be developed and transmitted from one generation to another for the good and posterity of the African cultures and identities remains critical. Besides, it should be always known by Mozambique and other African societies that a dead culture entails a dead society for people are a People because of their culture: people without culture are like trees without roots.

Chapter 2

Decolonising African literature: An unfinished business

Introduction

There is monumental literature by philosophers like David Hume, George W.F. Hegel, Immanuel Kant, Lucien Levy-Bruhl and Diedrich Westermann, among other theorists and anthropologists, that describe Africans as *tabula rasa* – a people with no reason/rationality; hence without a history and worse still philosophy. Westerners considered Africa as a dark continent (Winch 1970; Churchland 1984; Ramose 1999; Mawere 2010). Other scholars such as Emil Ludwig, even described Africans as a people with no religion and philosophy but culture. Ludwig (cited in Awulalu 1991: 125) tacitly exclaimed: 'How can an untutored African conceive God? ... How can this be? Deity is a philosophical concept which savages are incapable of framing'. Many Euro-centric scholars, thus, despised Africa's traditions, customs, belief systems and indigenous knowledge systems as diabolic, barbaric and primitive. It is unfortunate that such myths have been continually recycled by racists and Euro-centric scholars even in the present times. Recently, in South Africa, for example, it was revealed that there are still many people of European descent who still believe that [indigenous] Africans are a race next to monkeys and baboons. It has been revealed by Free State-South Africa, Correspondent, Mogomotsi Selebi, in *The Sowetan Newspaper* (4/10/2013) that:

A white Free State teacher, Leornard McKay of Wilgehof Primary School asked black pupils to look into a mirror and told them that they were seeing baboons ... McKay is allegedly said to have said black people had monkey-like noses and primate brains ... A report by the South African Human Rights Commission (SAHRC) states that 'McKay's act of hate speech constitutes clear violation of both the right to equality and the right to human dignity of the learners'. The commission also noted that the other 26 white teachers also showed racist tendencies by their refusal to cooperate with the department. This was after all of them refused to fill out the questionnaires sent by the commission about racism at the school. Only the six black teachers complied (pp. 10).

Such actions is a clear manifestation that some false and pejorative images still exist in the minds of many of some of the people of European descents, unfortunately even among some of the latter born and bred in Africa. This false and pejorative label have always had (and will continue to have) a negative impact on the African people and Africa's own socio-economic and political development. It is one reason, among many others, that during the colonial era Africa's valued traditions, knowledge systems and philosophy of life had to change to fit in with the Western scientism and the so-called [Western] modernity. Authors of the time had to write in a way and style that pleases the White colonial administrators as anything against the colonial regime was far from being tolerated. This way of doing things came as a fatal blow and drawback to Africa and the African people.

Fortunately, some creative works by some [indigenous] African writers have captured the true imagination, epistemology and axiological systems of Africa. Yet it remains a surprise that using the theme of characterisation, some African writers have misrepresented the African values and traditions in their literary works. On the other hand, scholars in the field of Philosophy have not devoted adequate time to analyse philosophical themes that run through African literature. They have left this business for creative writers. It however remains a critical question whether this should be a game for creative writers alone.

As they seek to proffer solutions to postcolonial Africa's problems such as poverty, neocolonialism, cultural decadence and the split-personality crisis, many of the leading writers such as Chinua Achebe, Ngugi Wa Thiongo, Okot p'Bitek, Mongo Beti, Patrick Chakaipa, Solomon Mutswairo and others have used the theme of characterisation in their engagement with modernity and Christianity. Using the theme of characterisation, these writers have tussled with the following questions in one way or another: "Why and how was Christianity brought to Africa? What was the impact of Christianity on the African culture? Is modernity compatible with tradition? How globalisation has impacted the non-Western societies?"

Though giving more emphasis to Zimbabwean first generation literature particularly Patrick Chakaipa's *Rudo Ibofu* (Love is blind), this chapter provides a preliminary analysis of the well thought literary device, 'characterisation' as it runs throughout the whole terrain of African literature (both written and oral/orature). The chapter presents an effort to open African literature to cross disciplinary work – to share with other disciplines like philosophy, sociology, development studies, and anthropology. While it acknowledges the fact that some novels by African writers 'present accurate and lively pictures (through characterisation) of the conflict between traditional African values and those carried to Africa by Europeans and North Americans' (McCarthy 1991: 152); the chapter points out the failure of some writers to accurately depict the relationship. They have described the relationship between African traditional values and Western ones in a way that is damaging to Africa; a way that jeopardises and threatens

Africa's wellbeing. In Zimbabwean literature, this is more vivid in the first generation creative writers.

The failure by most first generation African creative writers to demonstrate a balanced relationship between Western values and the indigenous ones is predicated by the thorough censorship of writers' literary works during the colonial era. It is this observation that motivated me to write on a topic such as this.

In the light of the above stated observation, this chapter as with part of the objective of the book as a whole, seeks to provide a corrective to the Western gaze that negatively impacted the consciousness of most of the first generation writers and demonised Africa in ways numerous to mention. It reiterates that 'Europe's intervention in Africa was the beginning of the most nefarious images, the 'black labelling' of Africans and their *philosophies*. An African invented for European purposes could no longer serve the interests of its own people' (Asante 2001: xiv) as Europeans despised all African traditions, customs, philosophies and knowledge systems. Indigenous writers were encouraged to write works that through the literary theme of characterisation despised African traditional philosophies and justify the perpetuation of Western dominance over Africa.

The chapter, as with the mode of this book as a whole, is reactionary in the sense that it is responding directly to trends identifiable in African literature spheres. In the light of this, the chapter provides a corrective to the Western gaze that demonised Africa, and in particular the African literature, by advancing the view that Africans were without a history, worse still epistemological and moral systems. The chapter, therefore, contributes to the rationality debate on African literature; it is a deconstructionist and (re)constructionist effort reminiscent of the many aspects of the African people's struggles to control their own identity, literature, philosophies of life, society and destination.. In other words, the chapter, is a contribution towards cultural revival and critical thinking in Africa where the wind of colonialism (and most recently of globalisation) in the recent past has significantly affected the indigenous African peoples' consciousness.

More importantly, the chapter examines how critical the literary theme of 'characterisation' is in "African traditional literature, that is, characterisation was always used as a vehicle to inculcate moral and epistemological values that oriented the African child to the 'real' world". In fact, since time immemorial, characterisation was used in African literature (particularly orature) to carry forward African values and knowledge systems from one generation to another. Yet, while the African societies have always enjoyed and benefited from characterisation in their literature, a plethora of multicultural, axiological and epistemological problems brought forth by colonialism almost outweigh these benefits. With the advent of colonialism, the same literary device – characterisation entrusted by the African society as a didactic and moral vehicle was despised, downplayed and in most cases abused or employed to advance the interests of the colonial master. Characterisation in the Shona novel, *Rudo Ibofu* of Patrick Chakaipa is a fine example. In the novel, the author uses characterisation to despise his own traditional religion (African traditional religion) in favour of Christianity. The consequences are that a subtle misconstrued image of Africa can indirectly be perpetuated within the academic setting. In light of this observation, this chapter quests for an urgency of now; an 'African turn' where indigenous philosophies are instituted into the mainstream philosophy and the Western gaze on Africa is corrected. With this corrective measure effected, it is the author's fervent hope, in the words of Nzewi (2007:5), that: 'After the bombardment of the invading tornados of fanciful knowledge, the indigenous lore of life will yet revive with innately refurbished shoots, and fulfil again the human mission of the musical arts in original Africa, and edify Africa's mental and human posterity'.

Characterisation: An analysis

Http://en.wikipedia.org/wiki/character_arts, defines characterisation as 'the process of conveying information about characters in narrative or dramatic works of art or everyday conversation' which is, it is giving a distinctive expression to characters to represent, interpret or communicate certain values and messages to readers/audiences. The term has its derivation from the word character hence the need to define *character.* Etymologically, the term character derived from the ancient Greek word *"kharaktêr (χαραϰτήρ)"*, the earliest use in English, in this sense, dates from the restoration, although it became widely used after its appearance in Tom Jones in 1749 (Aston and Savona 1991; Harrison 1998) and in African orature since time immemorial. In literature (African literature included) a character is the representation of a person in a narrative or dramatic work of art such a novel, folktale, play, or film (Baldick 2001; Childs and Fowler 2006). It is a mode of communication or vehicle which conveys special messages from the author/narrator to the readers/audiences. This denotes that characters are the basis from which themes of a novel or work of art and intentions of the author are drawn. Since the 19thcentury, "the art of creating characters, as practiced by actors or writers, had been called characterisation" (Harrison 1998: 52). Characters may be presented by means of description, through their actions, speech, or thoughts.

Character development is very important in character-driven literature, where stories focus not on events, but on individual personalities. Classic examples in African literature include Solomon Mutswairo's *Feso* (Devil thorn) (1956); Patrick Chakaipa's *Karikoga Gumiremiseve* (The lonely one of the ten arrows) (1958) and *Rudo Ibofu* (Love is blind) (1961);

Ndabaningi Sithole's *Obed Mutezo: The Mudzimu Christian Nationalist* (1970); Stanlake Samkange's *The Mourned One* (1975), and Wilson Katiyo's *A son of the soil* (1976), among others. This paper adopts Patrick Chakaipa's *Rudo Ibofu* for the reason that he uses the devise of characterisation to denigrate (his own) African traditional religion; an error that the author of this works quests to correct. The author identify with Meki Nzewi (2007: 4) who strongly feels that 'contemporary Africans must strive to rescue, resuscitate and advance our original intellectual legacy, or the onslaught of externally manipulated forces of mental and cultural dissociation now rampaging Africa will obliterate our original intellect and lore of life'.

Also, Chakaipa's use of characterisation is vivid throughout his novel. Of interest is the way he eschews the political, hardly question the socio-economic system and tend to see social and political problems in terms of weaknesses of individual characters hence his being didactic and moralistic.

As said earlier on, historically, stories and plays focusing on characters became common as part of the 19th-century Romantic Movement and character-driven literature rapidly supplanted more plot-driven literature that typically utilises easily identifiable archetypes rather than proper character development. In African orature before colonialism, characterisation served mainly as a didactical mode to perpetuate Africa's indigenous knowledge systems and moral values. Even first generation writers continued to use characterisation as a didactical tool; but abusively as a tool to downplay African traditional religion and all traditional systems that belong to Africa.

The context of first generation Zimbabwean and African literature

The best way to appreciate characterisation in Zimbabwean literature is to locate the latter in its proper context, the African context. Contextually, Zimbabwean literature makes part and parcel of the whole terrain of the African literature, both written and oral (orature). While a detailed history of the development of Zimbabwean literature lies outside the purview of this article (Kahari, 1980), a number of issues need to be noted.

To begin with, 'Zimbabwean literature' is a multivalent term. It could refer to publications by white writers during the war (1972 to 1979), creative works in English and vernacular languages by black Zimbabweans (both inside the country and in diaspora) or any other expanded definition. However, the output by white writers has been properly ascribed to the Rhodesian novel (Chennells 1995). Significant authors like Dorris Lessing and Wilbur Smith, although contributing to the corpus of Zimbabwean literature, have an ambiguous classification since many regard them as British and South African writers (Malaba 1998). In this chapter, a restricted notion of 'Zimbabwean literature' is operational. The term Zimbabwean literature shall be used to mean both written and oral works of art in English and vernacular languages by black Zimbabweans (both inside the country and in diaspora). While the emphasis is made on literature written in Shona by Chakaipa, reference to some English novels is also made in an effort to minimize the exaggerated differences between Zimbabwean works in English and Shona. It is also critical to note that the development of literature in Zimbabwe, as indeed elsewhere in Africa, is intertwined with the nation's political and socio-economic history. The artists, especially the first generation writers are products of an education system in which missionary bodies had an important role (Siyakwazi 1995) though the missionary's major objective was to bolster a rise in conversions. One of the leading African nationalists and a first-generation Zimbabwean writer, Ndabaningi Sithole, celebrates the contribution of missionaries to the advancement of the Africans. Thus, 'it was the Christian church that first introduced literacy which was to give birth to the African nationalists, medical doctors, advocates, businessmen, journalists and graduates' (Sithole 1970: 98). Although nurtured by the missionaries, with the first four novels in Shona and Ndebele being published between 1956 and 1957, a salient aspect of early creative writing was the preoccupation with African cultural pride. These writers employ the device of characterisation to have their messages and intentions fulfilled. In his analysis of Samkange's *On Trial for My Country* (1966) and Solomon Mutswairo's *Mapondera: Soldier of Zimbabwe* (1978), the critic Zhwarara identifies the quest for recovering and celebrating Africa's past as a burning issue. Inspiring these two writers, he observes, 'is their desire to refute the White man's fraudulent claims that the Black man had no history and no culture to speak of' (Zhwarara 1987: 132). Like colonialism, it would appear the church in Africa had sponsored some of her fiercest critics, as is explicit in Solomon Mutswairo's *Mapondera: Soldier of Zimbabwe*.

However, some first generation writers like Priest-cum-teacher Patrick Chakaipa in his *Rudo Ibofu* (1961) uses the literary device, characterisation to denigrate African traditional religion. On one hand, this was because he was a staunch believer of the new religion – Christianity. On the other hand, this was because before the attainment of political independence in Zimbabwe in 1980 (like elsewhere in Africa), works that were explicitly critical of colonialism were heavily censored. Many writers were forced to dwell on 'innocent' topics such as love affairs, migration to the city and others that denigrated African traditional religion and practices. What remains interesting, however, is that all these first generation writers used the device of 'characterisation' to echo their messages and intentions to the readers who are in most cases young people. Due to its influence and literary powers to convey messages, the literary device of characterisation has gained homage even in contemporary Zimbabwean literature;

hence the need to briefly look at the 'literary powers' of characterisation.

Characterisation in Zimbabwean literature: Epistemological and moral aspects

Zimbabwe has 98% Africans of which the Shona constitute one of the largest communal-cultural groups. This group is an aggregate of small ethnic groups who are all classified as Shona because they each speak a dialect of what the linguists call the Shona language (Gelfand, 1973) followed by the Ndebele 16%, other African 11%, white 1% (Bureau of African Affairs, 2010). Since the Shona and Ndebele constitute the largest part of the population and for purposes of this work, Zimbabwean literature shall be confined to these two major ethnic groups. There is so much horizontal similarity across the spectrum of the ethnic groups that are classified as the Shona and Ndebele with those classified as other African ethnic groups, they share a common culture and most of the other ethnic groups also speak Shona. And what is distinctively African in Africa literature today and by extrapolation Zimbabwean literature derives from African traditional thought.

In this light, Zimbabwean literature like literature elsewhere in Africa, particularly oral (orature) and written by first generation writers share a number of features in common. Characterisation is one such feature. Before written literature, this literary device featured in orature especially in '*ngano*' (folklore). The term *ngano* is both in the singular and plural forms. The *ngano* tradition has a very long history in Shona culture. It dates back to the mythical origins of the Shona people. When Shona people speak of *ngano*, they refer to a unique genre of oral literature that is distinguished from other genres such as myths, legends and chronicles on the basis of its narrative structure, content, objective and aesthetic considerations. *Ngano* thus is a general term for any of the numerous varieties of traditional narratives or any of the above stories that are told orally in a particular community. It is curious to note that *sarungano* (story teller/owner of the story) intensively used characterisation in order to clearly usher the content, objective and the aesthetic considerations of the *ngano*. In *ngano* characterisation was not only a subject of aesthetic consideration but had positive epistemological, ontological and moral implications. Basically *ngano* portrayed the struggle between *dos* and *do nots* of a society, good and bad, virtues and vices. The dominant but latent motif in *ngano* artistic conventions was the quest for African identity through moral values and epistemological systems in her culture. The children and *sarungano's* traversing through events/plot of the story, besides being titillated by its beauty, was also a search for moral justice. Through characterisation, allegorical morality was often used with characters of good deeds always triumphing in the end. The peroration of the story was supposed to usher emotional relief to the audience by providing a suitable and satisfactory resolution to the story's moral struggles. From an Aristotelian persuasion, the ending of tragic *ngano*, for example, releases the audience from an emotional tension that would have resulted from the stormy events of the plot as the forces of evil and good were pitted against each other through characterisation. In other words, the ending should provide emotional therapy to the children/audiences through purgation that firmly stamped the African society's moral, ontological and epistemological concerns.

Epistemologically, children were equipped with knowledge of the physical environment and animals of the jungle through *ngano*. They (children) were furnished by the *sarungano* on what each animal character symbolised. Children were also taught the general behaviour of each animal and furnished with information and justifications on what it would mean to be considered 'this animal' in their society. For instance, Hare embodied wit and trickery; Baboon represented stupidity, naivety, artlessness, ugliness or cruelty; Lion stood for courage, aggression and power, he is the king of the jungle; Hyena represented selfishness and greediness, he had an insatiable appetite for meat; Monkey epitomised vigilance, agility and versatility and tortoise symbolised unnecessary slowness although he was also a symbol of unique wit that was normally used to counteract that of Hare. This use of characterisation was also meant to embrace and promote intelligence, rational thinking, hardworking, courage and vigilance in the young. Because of what they learnt from *ngano* and the *sarungano* the young would always attempt to account for their actions in real life. This attempt to provide justifications for their behaviour/actions was the beginning and manifestation of epistemological thinking in the African child.

Social life and knowledge on family relations were also taught through characterisation in *ngano*. Hare is called *Tsuro Magen'a* (Hare, The Cleverest/Trickster). *Gudo* (Baboon) who in *ngano* happens to be Hare's uncle (that is, brother of Hare's mother) is always at the mercy of his nephew's cunning behaviour. Not only are Baboon's pretty girls snatched away by Hare, he is always made the public's target of laughter by being lured into and left to be stung by wasps or bees. Thus through Hare's charismatic actions as well as the actions of other animal characters children and adults alike were filled with thrilling excitement, imagining and seeing their real life experiences being simulated by animals.

It is precisely for the teaching role with particular reference to a *sarungano* (who was usually a grandmother) that she was considered as 'an omniscient narrator in Luo culture' (Benedict and Adrain 1974: 25) and her hut (the *siwindhe*) an 'institute for cultural traditions and social preparation' (Benedict and Adrain 1974: 25) A *sarungano* was therefore a philosopher in the African context. She (*sarungano*) transmitted the philosophy of her culture to the youthful members of society while simultaneously shaping the same philosophy. Thus at the bottom of *ngano* and its artistic beauty was the thought system of African culture to which the oral artist oriented the people of her culture. It is therefore surprising that literary discourse on characterisation remains a game for creative writers alone; the reason why I argue, in this book, for the rehabilitation and restoration of indigenous African philosophies into the mainstream philosophy.

When the first generation writers started publishing in the 1950s, characterisation remained critical in their literary works. For various epistemological, axiological and moral concerns, first generation writers in Zimbabwe like Thompson Tsodzo, Solomon Mutswairo, Stanly Samkange, Patrick Chakaipa, Bernard Chidzero, extensively used the literary device of characterisation as shall be seen in the ensuing discussion.

Epistemological and moral implications of characterisation in Chakaipa's *Rudo ibofu*: Paying homage to Chakaipa's characterisation?

Here, the author starts by posing a crucial research question: What are the benefits of Patrick Chakaipa's characterisation to African literature?

A close look at Chakaipa's characterisation will set the tone for a philosophical exposition guided by the above research question. To this end, the article seeks to unravel characterisation in African literature, particularly Zimbabwe's first generation novel, *Rudo Ibofu* by Patrick Chakaipa. As previously underlined on the reason for choosing Patrick Chakaipa is that he contrasts the traditional use of characterisation in African culture; he uses characterisation in a way that stifles, strangles and denigrates traditional African religion and Africa's being of existence. Hence the present work seeks to challenge his position.

The use of characterisation by Chakaipa like any African creative writer is not accidental. Characterisation has been in

43

use in African literature particularly oral literature (orature) since time immemorial. As said earlier on, characterisation was not only a subject of aesthetic consideration but had positive epistemological and moral impact to the audience. Through characterisation, characters were used as modes of communication – vehicles which convey special messages from the author/narrator to the readers/audiences who are usually young people who are still to be inculcated with moral principles and epistemological systems. This denotes that characters are the basis from which themes of the novel and intentions of the author are drawn. However, the reverse in terms of the purpose in which characterisation was used for in African literature particularly in written literature seems to be the case in many first generation writers (not only in Patrick Chakaipa's *Rudo Ibofu*) of the third world countries where there had been a huge gap between the anticipated gains of democracy and the reality on ground. This trend is evident in Bernard Chidzero's *Nzvenga Mutsvairo* (Dodge the Broom) and Chakaipa's *Dzasukwa Mwana asina hembe* (1967: The Pots have been Cleaned for Beer Brewing) (1967). Those which tend to be more critical of the colonial situation are very few and exemplified by Thompson Tsodzo's *Pafunge* (1970: Think About It) and Aaron Chiunduramoyo's *Ziva Kwawakabva* (1976: Know Where You came From) and Solomon Mutswairo's *Mapondera: Soldier of Zimbabwe* (1978). Obviously, the state-controlled Literature Bureau established in 1953 as well as the influence of missionary teaching affected the nature and orientation of the Shona novel. The manipulation of characterisation by some African writers makes it critical to analyse each character featuring in a narrative in relation to his [her] name and immediate environment. The author argues along with Kahari (1986) that in order to understand characterisation in a novel, it is important to understand the linguistic philosophy of the author and the language she/he uses. As Kahari (1986:221) puts it: 'Characters are to be studied

44

by making a thorough critical analysis on their names, roles, their origins, place and justification for their existence and activities in the society concerned'.

In light of the above, Chakaipa in his *Rudo Ibofu* employs characterisation in a way that throws light on and makes readers to determine the message(s) intended. He uses *mazita emadunhurirwa* (nicknames) which clearly identify the characters with reality in the Shona culture and worldview – the names have meanings that can be drawn from the Shona people themselves. However, as a Roman Catholic Priest-cum-teacher, Chakaipa chiefly uses characterisation to inculcate in his readers the supremacy of Western religion (Christianity) over African traditional religion. This authenticates Kwasi Wiredu's (1996) observation that using African writers the White colonialists sought, sometimes somewhat successfully, to transpose or even impose their own fallible conceptions of religion, morality and life in general upon Africans. In fact, as a result of some ingrained ethnocentrism, the West had attempted to obliterate everything African and replace it with their conception of knowledge systems and moral values to be used in day-to-day life. The colonialists and early missionaries appointed themselves the haste purveyors of the universal Western culture, which for them represented a culture that every civilised society was to live by. And since the African encounter with Western modernity, indigenous African culture and everything African earned itself the designation tradition. In the colloquial sense, tradition remains old-fashioned, attached to the past, and unchanging, while modernity claims constant renewal, movement towards the future and continuous change (Brodnicka, 2003). As highlighted by Brodnicka (2003:1):

The usefulness of tradition to Europe was at least twofold: the first one is that the concept of tradition allowed Africans to appear backward, childlike, and natural as compared to their European counterparts and therefore suitable for domination, and secondly the concept of tradition also created the notion of ethnicities as different and threatening to each other's traditions.

For this reason, it was, therefore, necessary that one tradition particularly that which represented backwardness is buried for the harmonious existence of the seemingly antagonistic ethnicities. This is what generally befell most of the first generation African creative writers and by extrapolation Zimbabwean writers. Chakaipa using the character, 'Rowesai' (one who can make her parents bewitched because of her beauty) unapologetically attacks the Shona traditional religion by showing that Christians are always generous and live a blessed life whereas the traditionalists always suffer. The West needed the tradition-modernity dichotomy more than the African for it served the interests of the West more than the African. This explains why the Africans' and in particular Zimbabwean traditional belief systems and their own worldview have been under threat since the advent of colonialism. A few bad things that were seen being practiced by the Zimbabweans in the name of culture were enough to brand the whole indigenous culture anti-modern and, therefore, retrogressive. For this reason, White characters and priests in *Rudo Ibofu* are idealised as purely religious and kind. Zingizi, for example, is forgiven by his employer when he fails to prepare a meal for the employer. He is also given a gift of clothes by his White employer. Similarly, Father Avondale (a White priest) in Tsodzo's *Pafunge* is portrayed as caring and kind. He voluntarily educates and looks after a lonely deserted African girl, *Rudo* (love). This stereotype of giving Whites and priests a favourable disposition is portrayed by several African writers who went through missionary education like Chidzero, Mustwairo and

Zvarevashe, among others. This was one way of downplaying African traditional religion at the expense of Christianity.

As if this is not enough, African names are changed to English ones; 'a thing that is still commonly practiced in some African countries like Mozambique' (Mawere 2010: 17). In the latter, children's traditional names are changed to Portuguese as soon as they start their primary education or at the time they are issued birth certificates. This is the same as what happens in Chakaipa's *Rudo Ibofu* where Rowesai is renamed Anna soon after baptism. Likewise, Zingizi and Chiramwiwa (The dejected) are renamed Joseph and Maria respectively. It is the contention of this work that change of traditional names to Christian ones is not rebirth as the missionaries purported, but cultural dislocation denial of African existence. It is a failure of the Westerners to acknowledge the African thought system. I, therefore, identify with Nzewi (2007:4, emphasis original) who believes that:

> Irreverent and irresponsible abandonment as well as flippant change started when the human and cultural practices of the invaders from outside (especially during slave trade and colonialism) began to make insidious intrusions into the African's human and cultural psyche thereby dehumanising and underdeveloping Africa and the African people.

African epistemology, metaphysics and moral philosophy that synthesises all African experiences in order to achieve a coherent whole which gives a complete picture of African reality is, therefore, necessary and indispensable. It is because of such intrusions by Westerners that prominent African writer; Ngugi wa Thiongo was provoked to write his *Decolonising the Mind: The Politics of Language in African Literature* (1981) suggesting a decolonisation process for the African people even after colonialism. Failure to undertake a decolonising process is likely to yield no development to Africa. The author is, therefore, quick to concur with Mervyn Caxton's (Eade, 2002: xii-xiii) view that '[all] models of development are essentially cultural'. Development becomes a cultural construct and the basis for inter-cultural engagement, albeit on generally unequal terms. Caxton (Eade, 2002: xii-xiii) continues:

> When a people faces challenges from the environment which require responses and solutions, one of the functions of culture is to provide criteria which would enable a selection to be made between alternative solutions. This essential role of culture is usurped, and its capacity to provide adequate responses to development challenges is impaired, if the criteria used are ones that are external to the culture itself. This is what happens when external development models are exclusively relied upon.

It is in view of this fact that the author argue for cultural revival in Africa. African people have strong memories of their indigenous philosophies and local practices and this self-conscious knowledge motivates them as they rely heavily upon these concepts. Even their names are pregnant with meaning and a philosophy in itself. Denying them is, therefore, not only denying African philosophy but African existence. In this light, the author share the same sentiments with Father Placide Tempels (1945) who rightly observed that those who refuse to acknowledge the existence of black thought exclude blacks from the group of human beings.

Chakaipa also uses type characters to denigrate African traditional religion and belief systems. A 'type character is one who stands as a representative of a particular class, ideology or group of people' (Baldick, 2001: 265). The characters in August Strindberg's *Miss Julie* (1888) and Henrik Ibsen's *Hedda Gabber* (1891), for example, are representative of specific positions in the social relations of class and gender, such that the conflicts between the characters reveal ideological conflicts (Aston and Savona 1991). This trend is evident in *Rudo Ibofu*. Chakaipa uses the Christian character Rowesai and the African traditionalist Mutandawachingama (A stumbling block) to represent Christian ideology and African ideology respectively. In his characterisation, Christians unlike African traditionalists always triumphs in goodness and win victory over vice and calamities. Rowesai survives death from wolves and leopards in the wilderness. On the contrary, her father, Mutandawachingama, a staunch traditionalist who vehemently opposes the rapid spread of Western values and lifestyles fails to lead a happy life. He only achieved a happy life after repenting and become a Christian convert: Western civilisation is in fact mistaken for salvation in as much as English language fluency is mistaken for intelligence in the same text. In the same vein, Matakanure, a traditional healer is depicted as heathen – a trickster and chronic liar. This is further revealed in the description of his stature as a black (which in the Western world view is associated with evil), ugly thin man with long projecting teeth and a big stomach that resembles a pregnant woman. This description reveals his frivolous character. It is worth noting at this juncture that Chakaipa's use of characterisation is detrimental to Africa. This is because African religions and philosophy are inseparably intertwined and its strong bond is supported by Mbiti (1975: 12) who rightly points out that 'religion is part and parcel of the African heritage which goes back many thousands of years'.

In other subsequent Zimbabwean novels, even some contemporary ones, *n'angas* (traditional healers) are portrayed the same way as Chakaipa's Matakanure. Zinyimo and Madzumbunure, traditional healers in Father Ribeiro's *Muchadura* (You shall confess) and Tsodzo's *Tsano* (Brother-in-law) respectively have their lives in trouble in the end. All these authors have the same intention of painting black, through characterisation, the *n'angas* who are the pillars of African traditional religion and epistemological systems. The Africans thus are forced to question and relegate their own traditional religion and thought systems in favour of Christianity; Chakaipa and colleagues' intentions are, therefore, achieved through characterisation.

Using characterisation, Chakaipa is not only preaching Western religion to Africa, but Western imperialism: Chakaipa is doing a disservice to Africa and the African people. Through the characters, Zimunya (one who is fond of eating) and Zingizi (one who is thin as a wasp) who is later known as Joseph, Chakaipa preaches supremacy of the Western culture over the indigenous one. Zingizi who represents the Western ideology is an embodiment of cultural arrogance and racism, and have no scruples in tossing Zimunya (who represents the African ideology) in public. Besides, labelling him as greedy, Zimunya is portrayed as a vagabond, a chronic liar, heathen, lazy, dirty and bully. Chakaipa (1961: 9) further describes him as 'one who thinks with his veins' and whose attire resembles that of a madman. Thus as one who advocates Westernisation, Chakaipa picks up 'the myth of dirty Africans'. He elevates the hysterical White woman who hates and rebukes Zimunya for dirtiness, laziness and lying as the model of Western civilisation. Though Chakaipa's sermon on hygienic practices is welcome to Africa and Africans, the way he portrays it is derogatory to Africa. In this light, the chapter calls for a 'return of Africa' to value its traditions and knowledge systems. This is what Masolo (1995: 2) calls 'The call for a return to *the native land* – one of the many revolutionary expressions of the then rising black militantism, nationalism and Africanism ... to counter Westernism's arrogant and aggressive Euro-centric culture'.

The call is critical and urgent not only to Zimbabwe, but other African countries. In Zimbabwe, some subsequent creative writers have taken the same direction as Chakaipa; a situation that is resulting in 'identity crisis'. Bernard Chidzero is a fine example of those who follow Chakaipa's footsteps. In his *Nzvengamustvairo*, Chidzero portrays Samere (who like Chakaipa's Zingizi represents western ideology) who unlike Matigimu and Tikana (who both represent African ideology) as one who has been enlightened with modernity. Samere describes the traditional attire of Matigimu and Tikana as 'nakedness'. In fact, the character Samere is used as the mouthpiece of the author (Chidzero) in preaching modernity at the expense of tradition.

Thus one of the dominant motifs in Zimbabwe literature is how missionary education produced alienated individuals. It is charged that they sought to promote an elite class that would despise Shona culture and consider worthless/inferior all those who remained attached to tradition. Ndatshana in Samkange's *The Mourned One* (1975) represents such a character. Raised at the mission station by the Methodist missionaries, he fails to adjust to the reality of village life in his real home. Having been pampered at Waddilove, with a full breakfast being a daily experience, the coarse mealie-meal porridge of his mother's kitchen is unsettling. It is, therefore, clear that missionaries have not prepared Africans to face the world as Africans but to look down upon and despise African systems and values. In fact, they brought an alien system of values. Africa was, therefore, robbed, raped, abused, exploited, manipulated, and above all, made to feel ashamed of her alleged worthlessness. This is not a light and negligible issue. It raises serious ontological, moral and epistemological questions. Thus, in view of Chakaipa's characterisation and that of many other writers discussed in this work, the author argues that such 'conditional and abused characterisation' cannot find homage in African literature or African philosophy in general. It is a result of some indigenous Africans (that is, people of African descent and those who take Africa to be their home) who have been radically impacted upon by colonialism to the extent that they are confused as to who they are. The author, therefore, advocates for a paradigm shift from 'conditional characterisation' to a 'comprehensive characterisation paradigm' that fosters objectivity, sensitivity and universality; characterisation that does not offend, denigrates, undermines and threatens to swallow the existence of the other (races).

Concluding remarks

With many internationally accredited African philosophers like Mbiti, Wiredu, Serequeban, Henry Odera Oruka, P.J.Hountondji, and the local [Zimbabwean] philosophers, it is surprising that many of them had little to say on the role of characterisation in the African way of life –'African philosophies'. The discourse on characterisation in African literature (oral and written) has been mistakenly considered a game for creative writers alone.

This chapter has demonstrated how critical characterisation was used in African literature as an element of epistemology, morality and African philosophy in general since time immemorial. More importantly, the study has shown how the same literary technique has been abused by those who wrote to please colonialists and missionaries. The mode of this work has been reactionary in the sense that it has been responding directly to trends identifiable in African literature spheres mentioned earlier in this work. It is, therefore, critical that scholars in philosophy and other disciplines engage in dialogue with some creative writers discussed in this article – some who through characterisation have misrepresented Africa.

The chapter has further argued that with the tide of colonialism and globalisation that has blown across Africa, the work of the African creative writer is becoming more and more complex and challenging yet the African writers should not be left behind by this global tide. African creative writers and experts in the field of philosophy and other disciplines should work (hand in glove) and even harder to ensure that African philosophies through literary devices like characterisation, for example, are not only correctly represented and removed from the backseat position, but are rehabilitated and developed to full bloom. Rehabilitating and developing such epistemological and axiological systems would allow young and emerging African philosophers to restore Africa's humanity, philosophise in context and apply philosophy in analysing and solving their daily problems more easily.

Finally, the virtue of this chapter has been to provide a corrective to the 'Western gaze', false and pejorative label that demonised Africa through the 'abuse' of some (African) literary devices (like characterisation), and by advancing the myth that Africans were without a history, worse still a philosophy. The demonization of Africa has the consequences that a subtle misconstrued image of Africa can indirectly be perpetuated within the academic settings, the world-over. In this light, the chapter has criticised, dismantled and challenged the inherited colonial legacies which have injured many African scientists and researchers' consciousness. The chapter is not only against the vestiges of colonialism, but of neo-colonialism and cultural arrogance perpetuated through literary works by some scholars. It is a reclaim of rationality and dignity for Africa through the restoration and rehabilitation of 'African indigenous philosophies' into the mainstream education curricula (formal or informal).

Chapter 3

(Re) writing Africa: The rhetorics of representations and Western-biased women and children's human rights in Africa

Introduction

Shocking numbers cited by Mpumalanga Education MEC, Reginah Mhaule shows that 1565 schoolgirls were reported pregnant between January and May 2013 compared to 1602 recorded for the whole year in 2012 ... In Gauteng Province, 4217 of 1 040 760 schoolgirls became pregnant in 2011 ... In KwaZulu Natal, 1800 schoolgirls were recorded to have fell pregnant between January and May 2013 ... North West education MEC Louisa Mabe revealed that in 2012, 1792 schools from grades 7 to 12 fell pregnant ... In Western Cape, 2458 schoolgirls fell pregnant in 2012 as compared to 2097 fell pregnant in 2011 and 2108 in 2010. According to 2009 report by the Human Sciences Research Council on behalf of the department called Teenage Pregnancy in South Africa, in total 59 436 pupils fell pregnant that year ... Statistics released by the national Department of Health revealed that 94000 schoolgirls across the country fell pregnant in 2011 (Sowetan Newspaper, 27 May 2013, pp. 2).

On the same year, another shocking story hits the South African media. The controversial story whose headline read: *"Top court gives go-ahead to kids as young as 12!"* revealed that:

South Africa's top court made it legal for children as young as 12 to have sex. The ruling means teenagers between the ages of 12 and 16 need no longer fear legal consequences if they engage in sexual activity ... The Constitutional Court said, in effect, that children of that age were having sex anyway! It

55

declared sections 15 and 16 of the Sexual Offences Act, which criminalised kissing, petting and penetration between young teenagers, to be unconstitutional (Daily Sun Newspaper, 4 October 2013, pp. 1).

The first extract reveals that already there is cultural and moral crisis in the South African societies. Given such a scenario as the one revealed in the first extract, it becomes even more worrying to find out that South Africa is granting sexual licence to children as young as twelve. Questions that arise are: "If young children as young as 12 are granted sexual licence, is this not going to impact negatively on their academic life and even their future?; Isn't such a licence a big diversion from African, and in particular South African, cultural values?; Isn't that granting sexual rights to children as young as 12 is likely going to further retard Africa's socio-economic development?" Worse still, 'traditional Africa abhors the idea of unwed mothers, pre-marital sex and public romance either by married couple or unmarried partners, the phenomenon of foster homes and the presence of street children' (Obioha 2010: 6). To this effect, even dressing that reveals one's sensitive body parts (especially for women) is detested and considered a vice. Two critical questions that arise in view of the above extract, therefore, are: 'To what extent does allowing children as young as 12 to engage in sexual activities guarantee the African traditional values responsible for moral decorum and rectitude among children? and, 'To what extent does the South African judgement passed on children help to foster and advance the cherished and highly valued African virtues of desisting from pre-marital sex?'

In this chapter, these questions, among many others, are critically discussed in view of children's human rights in Africa and in light of Westernisation and globalisation. An analysis of the impact of Westernisation (since colonialism in Africa) and of the current wave of globalisation is, thus, discussed in terms of how Westernisation and the so-called globalisation (i.e. with their Western-based conception of women and children's rights) have impacted the African culture, morality and socio-economic development.

The spreading of human rights ideology with focus on Africa

Stereotypical thinking of Europe over Africa and the African people has never been neutral: it had emotional content and commonly associated with attitudes of hostility and hatred towards Africans. Though there was nothing natural the opposition between white and black in other cultures, in European cultures this symbolism was indeed pregnant with meaning. White (representing Europeans) and black (representing Africans) was, therefore, deeply rooted in European culture, and with negative labelling of the African people by the Europeans. White was, for instance, associated with purity and black with evil. This is aptly captured by Joel Kovel (1970: 62) who noted:

> For Europeans, the symbol 'blackness' held the following meanings before the West came into extensive contact with Black peoples: 'deeply stained with dirt; soiled, foul ... having dark or deadly purposes, malignant; pertaining to or involving death, deadly; baneful, disastrous, sinister ... indicating disgrace, censure, liability to punishment.

In the language of scholars such as David Hume, Immanuel Kant, Hegel, and Levy-Bruhl, among others, Thomas Jefferson similarly wrote of the 'black' people that: 'in memory are equal to whites; in reason much inferior; in imagination they are dull, tasteless and anomalous' (Gossett 1963: 42-4). The symbolic meanings of 'black' and 'white', thus, influenced European reactions to the African people who they labelled 'black' when the former encountered the latter on

African shores. Such ideas, which are credited to the father of modern racism, Count Joseph Arthur de Gobineau (1816-1882) influenced the thinking and attitude of many European people (such as Adolf Hitler) towards the Africans. Gobineau, for instance, proposed that there exist three races: the white, black and yellow with the white possessing moral reasoning, intelligence and generally superior to the other two races.

Although some Europeans thinkers have debunked this eurocentricism, yet and surprisingly, many still hold on to the notion of superiority of the white although totally without factual value or empirical validation, remains a key element of white racism even today. It is, therefore, curious, especially for African critical thinkers, to see the very people who until recently have been involved in the nefarious projects of slavery and colonialism all over Africa purporting to be rescuing Africa from the mercy of violation and abuse of other people's human rights. Is this proposal of the Universal Declaration of Human Rights of 1948 — a document drafted at the height of colonialism in Africa — really a genuine proposal? Before discussing this question, let us review the background of human rights in Africa in general.

Traditional African way of life (egalitarianism) is holistic as it enmeshes together values and people through concrete constitution. This is directly opposed to the Euro-centric way of life that is normally driven a tendency toward isolation of the other (e.g. the African) and individualism. The structures which slavery and colonialism as well as its twin sister, apartheid had built over the last five centuries reveal who the former colonialist is in relation to human dignity and the respect of human rights. I argue in this chapter that these structures though have been abolished and now visibly absent are still existent as they have been reshaped and conveniently renamed. This is because systems that discriminate, segregate, dominate, and violate human rights and dignity continue to exist across the globe. Worse still, most of these systems are perpetuated by the West and America, countries which see themselves as the architects of democracy and good governance. I can give an example of the Human Rights Watch (HRW) to show the hegemonic and domineering tendencies of some European countries and America. One would be surprised to note that: 'Human rights watch is founded on the idea that the values of the United States are universal, and that the US must impose them on the rest of the world. As the largest human-rights lobby, it is partly responsible for the increasingly expansionist US foreign policy' (Treanor 2008, http://www.antiwar.com/rep/treanor1.html). Some penetrating questions can be raised here: "By what virtue does the US have the right to impose its own values/ideologies on the rest of the world?" "Isn't it that the HRW is implying that the Americans are more human and rational than all others in the world?" Whichever way, I find it convenient to point out that such a belief by America that she is the "god" of the world is extremely dangerous: it is a belief that should be castigated into the dustbin of oblivion to be forgotten once and for all.

Putting that aside, I find it imperative to note that besides the colonial project that was instituted on Africa in the false name of civilisation and the HRW lobbied in the name of love for peace, the establishment of the 1948 Universal of Human Rights Declaration (UHRD) revealed the double standards and hidden agendas behind many projects on Africa especially from the North. Prior to the establishment of the UHRD, there was little evidence gathered by scholars and theorists that showed lack of honest and good faith behind most of the external projects in Africa, particularly those from the North. Since the 1960s, Afro-centric scholars and theorists have gathered and continue to gather evidence around the aforementioned claim. Molefi Kete Asante, for instance, has demonstrated how Europe has stolen and sometimes misrepresented philosophies from and by [indigenous] African people. In his most cherished literary work, *Things fall apart*, Chinua Achebe has shown how in the name of civilisation, colonialism was established in Western Africa and many other parts of the continent. So is Ngugi Wa Thiongo and Walter Rodney who have respectively argued for the decolonisation of the African mind, and demonstrated how Europe (and subsequently America) are held responsible for having underdeveloped Africa and indeed continue [even today] to economically and politically disempower Africa and the African people. It is indeed in view of these realisations that one would see no reason of embracing organisations such as the HRW and UDHR without question as it is apparent that most of these documents are only meant to advance and impose certain elite countries' ideologies or values on the rest of the world: there are hidden motives behind their founding such as protecting the rights of the rich especially those that got their riches through exploitation of other peoples. Based on the aforementioned observations, I argue that both the HRW and UDHR are not documents of peace as they promote war in the name of military intervention [or ideology of interventionism] as justification to protect the innocent. Also, they are not documents of equality as they have some elements of universality and superiority which make most Europeans and Americans to think that they are superior to all others in the world. Unfortunately, the non-Euro-American societies seem to have accepted these documents without question. I insist that there is need to subject these documents to critical analysis before embracing them wholesomely. In fact, there is need for non-Euro-American countries to counterbalance Euro-American political, social and economic dominance by lobbying for the increase in political and economic space of developing countries such as many of those in Africa.

Historical events have helped reinforcing findings by critical Afro-centric scholars about how Europe and America are "playing" the rest of the world. The establishment of the UHRD in 1948 by the United Nations (UN) (including

Western powers) is a case in point. In the very year the UHRD was established the Afrikaner Nationalist Party, proclaimed apartheid (meaning separate development) as the official policy of the South African state: apartheid was a policy invented in Britain and later exported to Australia and the United States of America. This was in spite of the fact that at the drafting and signing of the UDHR, South African Prime Minister, Jan Smuts and a team of South African white lawyers represented all of Southern Africa.

Besides apartheid, imperialists were well known for cruelty. Ben Kiernan (2007: 368-69), for example, detailed the brutalities, destructions, and annihilations perpetrated by the French troops to the Algerians in the city of Constantine in the nineteenth century:

> The French troops bombarded and attacked the town of 30,000, leaving corpses of the inhabitants strewn 'everywhere on the ground. The threshold, the courtyard, the stairs, the apartments, all these places were covered with bodies so close together that it was difficult to take a step without treading on them. And what to say of this trail of bodies on the torturous contour of the precipice where the unfortunate women had tumbled with their children on being seized with fright at our entry into the town.

In another horrendous incident, V. G. Kiernan (1982: 163) records that 'the worst in the conquest of Algeria occurred in 1845 and made a great stir at the time. A force led by Pélissier trapped some five hundred men, women and children in the Dahra caves, and kept fires burning at the entrance until they were all suffocated'. In South Africa, the British:

> Launched a wave of aggressive wars that would decide once and for all that Britain and its Cape Colony were the ultimate owner of these newly found riches of South Africa

... In 1873 the British made war against the Hlubi; and in 1877 against the Gcaleka and the Pedi; and against the Ngqika, Thembu, Pondo, Griqua, and Rolong in 1878. The Zulus were next in 1879, the Sotho in 1880, the Ndebele in 1893, and the Afrikaner republics in 1899. The Cape absorbed the Transkei and its peoples during the period 1879-94. Prior to that, Britain had annexed Basutoland in 1868, Griqualand West in 1871, the South African Republic in 1877, Zululand in 1887, Matabeleland in 1894, and the Afrikaner republics in 1900. The Zulu rebellion in 1906, in which nearly 4,000 Africans were killed, marked the last stage in 250 years of armed struggle by the traditional societies against white invaders (Magubane 1996: 53).

Elsewhere in Africa, for example in Namibia, German troops were involved in genocide when they killed the Herero people after the German commander issued out an Extermination Order. As recorded by Kwame Opoku (2014: 12) the Extermination Order read: 'Any Herero found within the German borders, with or without a gun, with or without cattle, will be shot. I no longer receive women or children. I will drive them back to their people or order them to be shot. These are my words to the Herero people'. Some years after this genocide was carried out by German against Namibia, and with the Universal Declaration of Human Rights in full force, German remains adamant to render a serious and official apology. Besides, the German state seems unwilling even to accept the need for compensating the unbearable suffering and damage inflicted on the Namibian people during the genocide which has best been known as the twentieth genocide in Africa by German. And, to complicate the matter even further, the German government has transferred the Namibian human remains to other Cultural Heritage institutions so as to erase direct and concrete proof and subsequently evade responsibility in the matter of the Namibian human remains.

For instance, human remains from former German colonies and other overseas territories such as Australia that were previously housed by the Berlin Museum of Medical History at the Charite Hospital have since 2011 been transferred to the Prussian Cultural Heritage Foundation. All this has been done in an attempt to rub away concrete evidence that the human remains were acquired in an unethically acceptable manner from the Germany colonies, and to consequently avoid an official apology, compensation and the handing over of the human remains by a high German government official.

In many other parts of Africa and beyond, even tougher racist legislations followed the proclamation of the UDHR in 1948. Since this book focuses on Africa I will give more examples from the continent. In Zimbabwe, for example, as late as 1965, the white settlers in Zimbabwe (the then Rhodesia) felt so insensible to the UDHR that they borrowed the apartheid examples of 1948 and 1961 in their declaration of white independence against African self-determination, a racist proclamation otherwise known as the Unilateral Declaration of Independence (UDI as opposed to the UDHR). In South Africa, many other examples are abundant. The Railways and Harbours Act of 1949 – an Act that segregated both passengers and workers on ships along racial lines – was, for example, established by the White South African government. In the same year, 1949, the Prohibition of Mixed Marriages Act of 1949 was added to the Immorality Act of 1927 targeting the black race that they would not marry with the white race. In the year that followed, 1950, the Suppression of Communism Act was introduced. This equated African aspirations for liberation with communism and legitimised the total denial of African aspirations for liberation in terms of the United States of America Cold War ideology. In education, the Bantu Education Act was introduced in 1950. This was meant to deny equal education between white and black and quality education to all Africans. Contrary to the 1948 UDHR, the Race

Classification Act or the Population Registration Act of 1950 brought to South Africa and indeed other countries where Cecil John Rhodes had some influences, the practices of racist population classification and discrimination which the British and the North Americans had just condemned and punished in Nazi Germany. Many other racist and segregatory legislations such as the Group Areas Act were introduced in 1950 and subsequent years. The aforementioned Act, for example, required racially classified individuals and groups to be forcibly removed from their respective according to the settler state's classifications.

The establishment of such repressive and discriminatory laws by the same people purporting to be promoting human rights for all the people in the world raises critical questions on the double standardness of the Western imperial countries especially when dealing with Africa and the African people. One would seriously ask: "Why and how could the same imperial countries (or their representatives) well known for snuffing out and violating other peoples' human rights or rather countries that have (and some continue to) commit[ed] horrendous crimes against humanity especially on the African continent call in very loud voices for the respect of human rights?" "And, why a call for human rights only now after several centuries of terrorism and snuffing out of the African people's freedom?" I should be quick to say that there is no doubt that the West could be charged of playing the role of a wolf in sheep's clothe by masquerading as the champion of human rights and yet is the hardest-boiled abuser of other people's rights. Such historical accounts (including the slavery and colonial projects) have prompted and made it a must for many African critical scholars and politicians to be always careful when dealing with the West. Though human rights are a universal concern for all human societies, others have lost total faith in the whole UHRD as they see nothing but an empty document that is nothing more than deceit. This in itself calls for scholars and politicians alike to, at least, revise some of their theories and claims on Africa in a way that would restore a sense of honest and faith of the African people on the North, even with development agents such as non-governmental organisations (NGOs) from the North.

Yet still far from repenting as it appears, the West and America, through massive donor funding, have since the 1948, through NGOs and other such institutions, encouraged African countries to celebrate the UDHR annually and every decade. In many African countries such as Mozambique, South Africa, Zimbabwe, Zambia and Malawi, among others, academics especially from the West and the Americas have produced pamphlets and academic textbooks since the establishment of the UDHR for use in educational institutions such as secondary schools, colleges and universities. Worse still, most of these pamphlets and texts are not critical about the context of people from cultures other than the West but basically the regurgitation of other people's (mostly from the West and the Americas) vignettes, slogans and opinions. There is indeed no critical questioning of the practical effect and in particular benefit of the UDHR to many countries in Africa and beyond such as Israel, Afghanistan, Syria, Mozambique, South Africa, Sudan, and Zimbabwe, among others that continue to suffer violation of their human dignity while continue celebrating the 1948 UDHR. While the production and deployment of the referred pamphlets and texts could be interpreted as a positive move in promoting world peace, it could also be interpreted as the double standards of the West and the Americas – a propaganda that encouraged 'blind celebrations' among many African populations.

It is in view of the reasons and arguments elaborated above against the Western and American governments that the West and America have been criticised by critical scholars especially from the south for preaching the gospel they themselves don't follow. Others see the 1948 UDHR as a mere marketing propaganda devised by the West to outwit populations from other continents (such as Africa) and create as well as convey to them a false message that the UDHR was indeed the basis for African liberation and of all the rights enjoyed today by all the individuals, communities, nations, continents, and indeed the whole world. No wonder scholars such as the Dutch Political Scientist, Paul Treanor, has in his famous paper: *"Who is behind Human Rights Watch?"* argues that it is in fact a lie to call the UDHR a "universal" document. I argue with Treanor that surely the UDHR has never been a 'faithful' document that expresses the genuine human rights of all people in the world for the reasons that:

♦Immediate after the 1948 UDHR, many segregatory and racist laws were passed in Africa by white settler, most of whom were signatories of the UDHR. Cases in point are the many examples of the Acts that were passed in South Africa and Zimbabwe by the British (and Boers) settlers who in fact were signatories of the UDHR.

♦ It is historically true that the majority of the governments in existence during the time which the UDHR was formed had been set up under the military dictatorship of the countries that won the Second World War. This means that most of the countries, with the exception of only five states namely the USA, the UK, Mexico, Sweden, and Soviet Union, signed the document without force or outside pressure. In fact the whole thing was an initiative of the USA that has been strengthened by the Second World War.

♦ All African countries were either forced into signing the UDHR or represented by the colonial powers of the time including those in South Africa who immediate after signing the UDHR went on to formalise apartheid policies in South Africa. Practically, Africa and the African people were not even covered by the UDHR. This means that as far as the issue of universal human rights is concerned, the UDHR has unjustly been imposed on Africa.

♦The wars against Yugoslavia and Iraq were waged by the United States of America against the UN Charter and in the name of the UDHR. So is the war in the Afghanistan where the USA has ever dropped nuclear bombs on fully populated cities.

Treanor further argues that:

Far from 'claiming' the rights in the Declaration, most of the world population never even saw the text before it was approved [by the few states] ... No political process of any kind was available to the population of even the signatory states, concerning the text of the Declaration. It was purely an intergovernmental affair. No election was held in any country, with the text [of the UDHR] as an election issue. No referendum, or any other form of test, was held to approve the text in any country. There was no notification procedure of any kind, since the Universal Declaration is not a Treaty. Despite the rhetoric about individual and inalienable human rights, no individual ever formally consented to the document, as an individual. The United Nations never organised any consent procedure.

He added that:

There is no procedure for revision of the Declaration. There is no procedure for periodic reviews, let alone periodic re-approval [or reaffirmation] ... There is no independent appeal against its contents, or against the rights imposed, or against the application [or abuse] of the Declaration by the United Nations. Specifically, there is no independent appeal procedure against military action to enforce it [which has recently become subject to high-handed abuses]. If the UN [Security Council] decides tomorrow, that it is necessary to destroy [a country or a city] with a nuclear bomb, to enforce human rights, then no one can take any legal steps against this decision.

It is out of observations such as these that Treanor concludes that human rights as contained in the UDHR are neither universal (catering for all human races in the world) nor Euro-centric or Western European centred as they are not culturally specific but politically specific. I agree with Teanor that the human rights doctrine [as contained in the UDHR] is a classic political ideology conceived by a white male and racist ruling elite in the context of the twin fears of both communism and Afro-Asian revolution: it discriminated non-Western races and the White female. No wonder in 1776, Abigail Adams made a plea for improving the situation of women in in the United States of America. She wrote to her husband, John Adams, who had to become the second President: 'I desire you would remember the ladies, and be more favourable and generous to them than your ancestors....Remember all men would be tyrants if they could' (Rossi and Calderwood 1973, Cited in Giddens 1993: 182). The same plea was made by women in France (through the leadership of Marie Gouze) after the French Revolution in 1789. Inspired by the ideals of freedom and equality for which the revolution was fought, women formed several clubs and Gouze (who was executed in 1793) drew up a statement entitled: *Declaration of the Rights of Women* based on the *Declaration of the Rights of Man and Citizen.*

If women in France and elsewhere in the West were organising themselves for the cause of achieving equal rights between men and women or to revolt against their White men counterparts, what about those countries that had suffered the ruthlessness of Western imperialism after the demise of colonialism in Africa and other parts of the world? In fact, given the colonial history of Western imperialists (and subsequently the USA), there was fear by the aforementioned powers that Africa and Asia might rally and revolt against the

Western powers and the USA: there was indeed fear for Afro-Asian revolution which had the potential to cause a third world war, that is, a war between combined forces from Africa and Asia against the West and America. Hence, Treanor is right in arguing that the UDHR is a narrow white male political ideology that is both undemocratic and unethical. It is indeed in view of reasons such as these that I argue in this chapter that due to a compound of factors, especially the impact of Westernisation and globalisation on Africa, the conception of human rights especially women and children's human rights has been exaggerated. Children, for example, are enjoying more rights than they possibly deserve resulting in consequences as those revealed in the first extract in the present chapter. This is no doubt exacerbated by legal rulings such as those revealed in the second extract.

How Africa has been tricked on the issue of women and children's human rights

In the name of globalisation and UDHR, Africa has been used to serve and safeguard the interests of Europe and America for a long time now. The missionaries and later the colonial regime propagated the myth that there was no conception of democracy and worse still that of human rights in Africa. They in fact confused the African people's view of autonomy particularly African hostility toward individualism for hostility toward individuality and autonomy. Yet a closer examination of the African people's way of life reveals a great passion for democracy and autonomous existence both at individual and group levels. At individual level, one had the right to express his [her] opinion even during court hearings (at dare or court sessions) and elsewhere. On the same token, autonomy of the group as a whole (including widows, widowers, orphans, and physically challenged) was guaranteed through egalitarian systems that encouraged both personal industriousness and collective work in the form of beer work parties (*nhimbe* in Shona or *ilima* in Ndebele). The *nhimbe/ilima* were meant to guarantee the autonomy of the widows, widowers, and orphans so that they are not looked down upon by other community members simply because they are poor or have nothing to feed themselves and their families with. It is clear, therefore, that the seemingly championing of the recognition of human rights in Africa by the Western community and America is nothing more than a political gimmick.

While there are many areas where Africa has been short-changed and tricked by the aforementioned powers, this chapter focuses much on the issue of women and children's human rights. By human right, I mean a 'claim that people are entitled to make simply by virtue of their status as human beings' (Wiredu 1996: 157). The issue of human rights is worth discussing because it is currently topical and has been used by Europe and America to dismantle the African family institution and to cause a lot of civil unrest all over Africa.

Starting with women's human rights, there is ample evidence that the Western world is known for individualism. By individualism, I mean the behaviour or attitude that makes someone does things in his [her] own way without giving much value to the surrounding community or society. This kind of life has disintegrated the family institution in the West such that personal interests seem to override the interests of the family and by extension society as a whole. Now there is no doubt that where family institution and the society's interests seem to be prioritised and respected more than individual interests as in the case of many African societies, it is difficult to disintegrate the family institution. This is what the West and America realised after the Second World War and when many of the African countries begun to attain colonial independence from the West in the 1960s. The Western powers and America anticipated that with communalism and intact family institution in Africa, it was easy for the Africans to mobilise each other and revolt against the West and America in retaliation of the sufferings incurred during colonialism and the Second World War. There was need, therefore, to roll off some forces and movements all over Africa to ensure that reunion and mobilisation across the continent is disrupted. This is when the plan around women and children's human rights was hatched to give force on the 1948 UDHR.

To gain acceptance in African societies, the West and America, through non-governmental organisations (NGOs) made their way into the continent through feminists, divorces, single mothers, and scholars in this delicate area of feminism. The NGOs funded a number of projects and researches around the issue of women's human rights so as to create, through the voice of feminist scholars, a false impression that similar to the Western woman the African woman was all in chains and the oppression of her male counterpart. The West knew very well that given the fact that most of the single mothers and divorces have had failed marriages and readily believe that all African men are oppressors. It was, therefore, easier to sow their seed in these women to roll over the idea in Africa. In Zimbabwe, for example, this idea was readily accepted by and spread through feminist scholars most of whom were single mothers and divorces. It is in view of these important observations that one could argue that the whole issue of UDHR is dubious, confused and fallacious that was universally but uncritically by the Western imperial powers.

Although falling into decline after the 1920s, feminism burst into prominence again in the 1960s with its 'heat' wave sweeping across Africa in the 1980s and through the 1990s. With this wave, the whole continent was sent into pandemonium as women begun questioning the status quo especially the traditional division of labour in the African home. This, with the monetary economy introduced during trade with the Arabs and popularised by during colonialism in

Africa, forced most African societies to move away from their egalitarian system and follow some forms of capitalistic economies. Yet with their egalitarian system, Africans were not only able to respect the rights of their societal members (including women and children) but even to cater for strangers. This is aptly captured by Robin Walker. Walker, in his *Roots of Black History,* cites the following example from Mwene Mutapa, Zimbabwe, based on the writings of Portuguese archivist Antonio Bocarro:

> [The Mutapa] shows great charity to the blind and the maimed, for these are called king's poor, and have land and revenues for their subsistence, and when they wish to pass through the kingdom, wherever they come food and drinks are given to them at the public cost as long as they remain there, and when they leave that place to go to another they are provided with what is necessary for their journey, and a guide, and someone to carry their wallet to the next village. In every place where they come there is the same obligation, under penalty that those who fail therein shall be punished by the king (Walker, 1999: 106).

One would ask: how then could African be so kind even to strangers like Bocarro when they were cruel to their women and children? One could also notice that Bocarro misunderstood African egalitarianism to charity in Catholic Europe. He failed to understand that African egalitarianism was even the opposite of charity as provision of resources such as food, land and so on was also meant for the physically challenged and the aged. This misrepresentation of some African systems was pervasive during colonialism as the missionaries and white scholars misunderstood and sometimes deliberately misrepresented the African people. No wonder Eric Hobsbawm and Terence Ranger note in *The Invention of Tradition,* that the white settler regime in Africa invented tribes;

concocted customs and so-called customary laws; appointed paramount chiefs and demoted former kings; *redefined relations between African men and African women*; and *defined African communities as inherent, conflicting and primitive shards of humanity held together by the binding vice of 'civilised' white rule.* The white settler regime, thus, charged with the evil mind of destroying the African institution (and by extension the African society) in the name of women's human rights saw the redefinition of relations between the African men and African women as the starting point. The African men was considered an oppressor of the African women and the white settlers even after colonial independence of the African states continued with their cunning behaviour: they wanted to be viewed by the world as the liberators of the African women from the African men and children from their biological parents. Unfortunately, uncritical African feminist scholars helped spreading the myth that African women were indeed living in the bondage of the African women. Uncritical as they were, they failed to realise that prior to colonialism in Africa the African men and African women were living at peace and in harmony with each other. Each had roles well defined such that even children were educated to master their respective roles both at home and outside home as they grow up.

Most importantly, these feminist scholars failed to realise the fact that patriarch was really a Western practice and not an African practice as many Euro-centric seem to believe. In reality, there used to (and still) exist many African societies that were matrilineal. Cases in point include the Akan people of Ghana. As reported by Kwasi Wiredu (1996: 158):

> Because the Akans are matrilineal, the most important kinship group is the lineage, which may be pictured as a system of concentric circles of matrilineal kinship relation that, at its outermost reaches, can include people in a widely separated geographic region. ...Its innermost circle

comprises the grandmother, the mother, the mother's siblings, her own children, and the children of her sisters. To this group, with the mother as the principal personage, belongs the duty of nursing an Akan newborn.

Other examples of matrilineal societies in Africa include the Herero of Namibia, the Tonga of Zimbabwe, the Tshwabo of Mozambique, among many others. All these examples show that the African societies were at least never as oppressive of their women as the Western societies that were basically patriarchal. It is the myth that African societies were all patriarchal and had no conception of democracy and human rights that the Eurocentric and feminist scholars spread throughout the world to justify their launching of women's human rights and campaigns against African men's oppression of the African women. It is the same myth that Eurocentric scholars and the so-called advocates of children's human rights in Africa spread across the continent to justify their launching and campaigning against parents' abuse of children's human rights. Wiredu (1996: 169) dispelling the same myth had this to say of the Africans and in particular the Akan people of Ghana:

> Akan thought recognised the right of a newborn to be nursed and educated, the right of an adult to a plot of land from the ancestral holdings, the right of any well-defined unit of political organisation to self-government, the right of all to have a say in the enstoolment or destoolment of their chiefs or their elders and to participate in the shaping of governmental policies, the right of all to freedom of thought and expression in all matters, political, religious, and metaphysical, the right of everybody to trial before punishment, the right of a person to remain at any locality or to leave, and so on.

It is quite surprising and unfortunate that even some African scholars, theorists and members of the public have been brainwashed and cheated to think that before the advent of the white settlers in Africa, Africans had no conception of human rights, worse still that of women and children's human rights. The Editor of the now defunct Daily Gazette Newspaper of Zimbabwe is a case in point. On the 8th of March 1994, the referred paper published a sweeping opinion on human rights and gender relations in African societies before colonialism where it was suggested that:

> In Zimbabwe, like most other African societies, women had no status of their own beyond that of their husbands ... women were generally regarded as mere appendages of their husbands and had no entitlement to land or property ... However, there was a basic rationale to this; traditional wisdom nurtured over centuries was perhaps less ambiguous about the social responsibilities of the gender classes ... women, for their part, bore children and attended to the more routine chores such as tending to livestock, cultivating the fields and looking after the home. There was no conflict of interest then and everyone was happy with their particular role (Daily Gazette, 8 March 1994).

In the same paper, an article was published on the 10th of April 1994 entitled: *African culture collides with basic human rights.* The article caricatured the African people's belief systems and perpetuated the myth that in Africa there was no conception of human rights before the advent of colonialism or at least the contact of the West with Africa. It is quite disturbing when one finds such myths perpetuated by some Africans themselves. A number of questions could be raised against such claims: By saying that women in Africa had no status of their own, does the author mean that there never women chiefs, sub-chiefs, or headmen on the African soils? If women never had properties of their own before colonialism, who then owned properties such as the kitchen, *n'ombe youmai* (mother's beast paid during marriage of a daughter) and so on? In fact women had properties of their own including gifts from their sons-in-law, part of their daughter's *lobola* (bride wealth) such as *n'ombe youmai,* and separate farms or fields where they grew crops of their own choices every year. Husbands had no power over these properties and women chose how they wanted to enjoy the fruits of the properties. Even in polygamous families, each woman had her own separate farm or field (as well as equal collective labour of the extended family) besides the one in the name of the husband which was collectively owned by the whole family. Each married woman (including those in polygamous families) controlled all their harvests from their respective fields whose labour came through *nhimbe* or her own labour combined with that of her children (during those times when there was no *nhimbe*). The husband's own harvest was used only for special occasions, for instance, when there was famine or when the wives' food exhausted before the next harvest. Such harvests were also used for brewing ritual beer (*bira*), marriage celebrations and a host of ceremonies. I should make it clear here that though in the Shona society (as in many other African societies) once a woman is married she becomes a full member of her husband and children's family, she still retained her autonomy. Her autonomy was considered as residing in her blood such that the woman, though now a full member of her husband and children's family, she retained her *chidawo* (maiden surname). This means that a married woman was never completely engulfed by her husband's family simply because she was married. At her own parents' home, the [married] woman retained her several critical role as *vatete* (aunt) and in the event of the death of her father and all her brothers as *babakadzi*. If the woman belonged to a royal family, she would automatically become the ruler (*mambo[kadzi]*). In fact in pre-colonial Africa, there were many women chiefs, a clear testimony that democracy existed in Africa well before the advent of colonialism. It is actually the colonial government that usurped the powers of women and watered down their significance in society. In precolonial Zimbabwean society, for example, powerful women chiefs such as Nyamazana who toppled chief Chirisamhuru of the Rozvi Empire existed. Awuah-Nyamekye (2012: 74) reports that even as of today, some Akan societies of Ghana have women as chiefs . And in some cases women serve as Divisional Chiefs). Yet with the advent of colonialism, female traditional authorities who used to have a lot of influence in the Zimbabwean pre-colonial society began to sink into oblivion given that the colonial regime had no respect for female leadership especially chiefs. Schmidt (1966:99) captures this aptly when he observes: "African women were 'invisible' to the colonial authorities. Having accepted the idea that women were perpetual minors in society and presumably played no part in public life, administration officials assumed that they had no political function". To this effect, Makahadze, Grand and Tavuyanago (2009: 39), give lucid example of what happened to some women chiefs during colonialism in southern Rhodesia (now Zimbabwe):

> The colonial authorities saw no reason why a female traditional chief had to be replaced by another female candidate. In 1934, headwoman Mupotedzi of Honde Valley died and was not replaced by the administrators. The same happened after the deaths of headwomen Shezukuru and Kanganya of Manica Reserve. The democracy and the rights that the female functionaries enjoyed became a thing of the past.

All these examples show that it is not true that women had no status of their own and never had properties of their own in the African society. The author of the referred article in the

Daily Gazette also seems to be ignorant of the fact that in some part of Africa, there were matrilineal societies whereby women were the principal personages in the family. In the previous sections of this chapter, I have given a number of examples of such societies right across the continent of Africa including the Tonga of Zimbabwe, the Herero of Namibia, the Akan of Ghana and the Tshwabo of Mozambique.

I should add that the white settler (or rather colonialism) is the one who violated the women and children's human rights most than anyone else. This is because when the [white] settlers came to Africa they created cities. In the cities, the settlers required labour from the African men. While in many countries such as Mozambique, Zimbabwe, and South Africa, among others, were not willing to leave their families (women and children) to work for the white men in the urban areas, they were forced to do so by circumstances. In Zimbabwe, for example, a number of taxes payable only through labour or money were introduced by the colonial regime to make sure that the African men is forced to leave home and work in the urban area. Worse still, the African men were not allowed to take their women to the urban areas as [African] women were actually not allowed to leave in the urban areas. The taxes introduced included hut tax, cattle tax, and many others. I argue in this book that by forcing (directly or indirectly) the African men to leave their families (women and children) and work for months or even years in urban areas violated both the women and children's human rights.

More so, the myth that African men have always been aggressive when dealing with the African women has been exaggerated []. I should point out that married women's autonomy was not only that attached to their blood. It was even respected when it comes to bedroom affairs. Married men and women in many African societies (for example the Karanga of Zimbabwe and the Ndau of Mozambique) had two separate and indeed different types of bedrooms. One of these bedrooms was one that both husband and wife slept together when they wanted to engage in sexual activities. The other one was that where each one of them would sleep alone when there was need to do so. To show that women had their autonomy preserved, a husband had no right to force his wife to join her in their common bedroom as it was traditionally considered dangerous to force a wife in those circumstances. It was in fact commonly believed that a wife can only choose to stay away from engaging in sexual activities with her husband when she wanted to protect him from something that might harm him. Such instances included cases when a wife was in her menstrual periods and when a wife had cheated on her husband or vice-versa. If the husband suspected that her wife chose to stay away because of the latter, he was supposed to call a *dare remusha* (family court) to establish the cause of her denial.

In the case of children, these were said to belong to the whole community. For this reason, children enjoyed gifts from anyone in the society. In Shona they had the saying that: *Mwana mudoko ndimambo* (A young child is a king). This is because just like a king a child was loved and his [her] rights (including the right to be loved) respected. While children were loved by everyone in the society, when they misbehave even in the absence of their parents they would be disciplined by anyone in the society. In other words, every normal adult was a disciplinarian/corrector. This was to ensure and guarantee the perpetuation of solidarity, interdependence, and a highly ordered, peaceful and harmonious society.

Unfortunately, the above scenario is now history in many African societies. In South African, Mozambican and Zimbabwean public schools, for example, teachers are prohibited from disciplining children they teach. In fact, in these schools teachers/educators are, in the name of protecting children's human rights, prohibited from executing and administering corporal punishment on learners. Worse still, in other African societies, parents are prohibited by law from beating up or administer corporal punishment on their own children. All this is typically un-African considering the fact that in pre-colonial period, children received discipline from any elderly member of the society when they erred. This is because children were considered an asset for the whole society who was supposed to exhibit morally acceptable behaviour to ensure and guarantee a future peaceful and harmonious society. I argue in this book that the move away from such a traditional treatment of children is causing havoc in the African societies such as the beating-up of educators/teachers by school pupils/learners. South Africa which in fact is the receptive centre of Western ideology into Africa seem to be the most affected society in Africa, south of the Sahara. In 2012, the headline: *Pupils attack teachers* shocked many as it hit the media. In one case it was reported that 'the safety of teachers at schools is under the spotlight ... A 14-year-old Jim Fouche Primary School, Johannesburg boy allegedly beat his female teacher ... after she insisted that the pupil remove a jersey that was not part of the school's uniform' (Sowetan, 8 October 2013, pp. 5).

In another case,

A 17-year-old Grade 10 pupil at SG Mafaesa Secondary School in Kigiso on the West Rand, [...] claimed he drank a home brewed concoction called skelm gemmer before he went to school where he assaulted two female teachers. The female teachers were punched in the face, one of whom bled through her nose (Sowetan, 8 October 2013, pp. 5).

In yet another case, it is reported:

A Sasolburg High School deputy principal escaped death, allegedly at the hands of a pupil after a gun was put

80

to his head but failed to fire ... This revelation is part of startling details that have emerged on what really happened when a 15-year-old pupil allegedly shot one of his teachers in the leg on September 20 (Sowetan, 8 October 2013, pp. 5).

The problem of indiscipline and moral decadence especially among the school going age group is fast spreading in Africa south of the Sahara. In Zimbabwe, for example, a headline where two form four pupils at one High School in Bulawayo sparked outrage among readers in October 2014. In the case, it is alleged that two Form Four pupils at Sobukhazi High School in Bulawayo were suspended from school ONLY for two weeks after they were caught having sex in a classroom in broad daylight (Chronicle, 08/10/2014). It is further reported that this incident occurred two weeks after a Form Three pupil at the same school gave birth to a baby boy in a school toilet and tried to hide it. What could surprise many, however, was the 'punishment' – two weeks suspension – after such a grievous offense. Yet, it should be noted that the school administration had no other tougher punishment it could have administered on the misbehaving students given that corporal punishment at school (and even by parents at home) is prohibited by Zimbabwean laws, laws that were adopted from the West.

All these examples are a clear testimony that African societies, and in particular Southern African ones, are in a state of cultural and moral crises. This is aggravated by legislations which appear to be protecting children's human rights when in reality they are negatively impacting on the lives of the African youths and societies at large.

My arguments in this book, and in particular, the present chapter should not be interpreted to mean that Africa was a continent of perfect societies before the coming in of the white settlers. In fact, I should be quick to point out that while I admit that in Africa there have always been certain men (as there are also certain women) who abuse other people's rights (including women's human rights) and that there are parents who abuse children's human rights (sometimes their own children's human rights), my argument in this chapter is that such abuses were exaggerated by the white settlers, Euro-centric and feminist scholars. Just like any other human society in the world, there have (and will) always trespassers (men or women) who abuse other people's rights but at least such cases were indeed few before colonialism in Africa given that the African societies were mostly communal and opposed to individualism. Besides, well before the advent of colonialism in Africa and the establishment of UDHR as well as women and children's human rights, existed institutions that dealt with issues to do with violation and abuses of other people's human rights. Instead of the West, the Euro-centric and feminist scholars learning from these institutions (for example the dare-African law court) on how issues of women and children's human rights were addressed in the African context, they misrepresented and spread the myth that Africa had no laws to protect its own people especially women and children. This was all done with the intention to be viewed as the champions of women and children's human rights in Africa and most dangerously to destroy the whole fabric of the African institutions of family and society. This is because with the establishment of women's human rights, women begun seeing their men as enemies who always think and do nothing good for women. So were the African children. With the establishment of children's human rights in Africa, children began viewing their parents as oppressors and never as loving parents as has always been the case. It is in view of all these observations that I argue that the women's human rights and children's human rights in Africa were the white men's assault on the African people: women and children's human rights were just meant to disintegrate the African family institution to

82

replace the culture of communalism with the culture of individualism. The call for women and children's human rights in Africa, thus, was meant to misrepresent and trick the Africans as well as make the world think that the Westerners and Americans were the champions of human rights in Africa. For this reason, among many others, African scholars (including feminist scholars) should leave aside the habit of being gullible of everything from the West even if it is the worst for the African people to adopt.

Africa and the global north: In search of the African framework for a genuine human rights document for all

I should point out that Africa has not only been cheated around issues of human rights and in particular women and children's human rights, but in other important areas such as medicine and economic development. Since this chapter focuses mainly on human rights, I will give just a few examples around issues of economic development where Africa has been cheated or short-changed. This is to reinforce my argument above that Africa has, for a long time now, been cheated by the West and America to think that there has never been explicit concern of human rights especially women and children's human rights. As documented by Tom Suchanandan, an environmental legal expert in the National Indigenous Knowledge System Office under the Department of Science and Technology:

The African Union did an economic study in 2005 and it revealed at that time that Africa was losing between US$5, 6 billion and US$8 billion from the theft of its biodiversity ... Although it's difficult to quantify the losses, we can give indicators since 98% of patents held worldwide are held by developed countries while only 2 % are held by

India and other developing countries (Sifelani Tsiko 2012: 2).

A closer analysis of the above words shows that Africa is perhaps losing even more than US$8 billion cited by Suchanandan. No African country is free from the losses. Zimbabwe, for example, suffered losses to Switzerland in 1995. As recent as 2010, South Africa, recorded two accusations of bio-piracy. As noted by Regis Mafuratidze (cited in Tsiko 2012: 2):

The first 2010 South African bio-piracy case involved the illegitimate use of traditional knowledge surrounding the medicinal properties of pelargonium sidoides by Germany's Schwabe, and the second, the bio-prospecting on Honeybush and Rooibos by Swiss food giant Nestle without appropriate permits from the South African government.

The above is a clear testimony that though the Convention on Biological Diversity (CBD) of 1993 and Nagoya Protocol were put in place as instruments which control the fair use and benefit of biodiversity or genetic resources, it remains clear that there is no strict system or framework to monitor bio-piracy and to regulate activities of multinationals most of which are from the North. As such, multinational companies continue to make huge profits from Africa's biological wealth but are not willing to share them with the local communities who own the resources. This calls for an urgent crafting of a development framework for Africa by Africans themselves to ensure that the continent doesn't continue losing millions of dollars to many Western countries and America. Here genuine bio-piracy laws that protect poor [indigenous] communities should be put in place to police those countries or companies with exploitative tendencies.

Now on the issue of human rights, which is the central focus of this chapter, there is no doubt that many African societies are already facing a cultural and moral crises as far as

84

the limits of human rights and in particular women and children's human rights are concerned. That being the case, there is need for Africa to re-think the whole question of women and children's human rights as postulated by the West and America. What is in fact most appropriate is Africa as a continent should come up with its own framework on human rights that [African] context based given that:

i). There were no African representatives except African colonial regimes when the UDHR was established in 1948. As I indicated earlier in this chapter, only representatives from South African colonial regime who unfortunately championed apartheid at same time UDHR was formed participated in the establishment of the UDHR. This makes it clear that the UDHR could be seen as a declaration that was meant to advance and pursue the Western imperial countries' own interests.

ii). Some of the clauses contained in the UDHR and its subsequent women's human rights as well as children's human rights seem to contradict with Africa's cultural values yet they are universally applied. I have demonstrated in the preceding discussion that clauses contained in children's human rights such as that to do with the administration of corporal punishment on children is contrary to Africans' worldview on issues of human rights. This is because most of the traditional African societies believe that if you spare the rod you spoil the child. I add here that the denial of administering corporal punishment on children (both at school and home) is more of a self-contradiction even among those countries that see themselves as champions of children's human rights and human rights in general. In fact, to the best of my knowledge there is no country without prisons or correction services departments. If corporal punishment is illegal on children, why then should it be legal on adults or at least why do we continue having prisons (which like corporal punishment inflict pain on the perpetrator) even in those countries that see themselves as technocrats of democracy and children's human rights? Isn't it that prisons (just like corporal punishment) should continue existing so as to protect other people's human rights and to serve societies from possible disharmony and confusion by 'bad apples'? Isn't it that only an 'ideally perfect' society is the only one where corporal punishment and even prisons should not be found? Isn't it the abolishment of corporal punishment and the laws against sexual activities between children that is causing thousands of teenage pregnancies in South African primary and secondary schools today? Isn't it the abolishment of corporal punishment that is resulting in teachers being assaulted by their own students in many schools across Africa today given that the minors know for certain that no legal consequences will follow?

In view of the above, I conclude in this chapter that the first thing to note in Africa is that we have a real problem as far as the issues of UDHR and women as well as children's human rights in Africa are concerned. The truth is that some African scholars who deal with jurisprudence, anthropology, philosophy and other such disciplines have not yet realised this. As suggested by Wiredu (1996: 5): 'the next desideratum is to try to test philosophical formulations in a metropolitan language in our vernacular to see if they will survive independent analysis. To do this is to try to decolonise our thinking'. Once it is realised it survives (which I am confident it does), a clear human right framework could be established by Africa based on the cultures in the continent before a comparison is done with the current UDHR which was in fact crafted by America and the Western countries.

86

Chapter 4

African indigenous knowledge systems (IKSs) and morality: Have African IKS run out of steam?

Introduction

> [...] communities and local practitioners use indigenous knowledge systems and practices to help increase their crop yields, educate their children, reduce suffering from HIV/AIDS, decrease infant and maternal mortality, heal the impact of conflict, learn from each other, and empower themselves (World Bank 2004: vii).

While there is wide acknowledgement of the [possible] contribution of indigenous knowledge systems at international level (e.g. the World Bank), it is still clear that its [IKSs) role in promoting moral rectitude in many [African] societies remains unrecognised or rather largely ignored. This is quite evident in the above statement by the World Bank. Yet the contribution of indigenous knowledge systems to the realm of morality in Africa cannot be underestimated. I underscore, here, that there is dearth of literature on Africa that demonstrates the contribution of IKSs in feeding the realm of morality and subsequently in promoting a harmonious, peaceful society. Most of the literature available around IKSs focus more on the possible contribution of African IKSs in protecting the ecosystem (Masaka and Chemhuru 2010; Mapara 2009; Mawere 2010, 2012), in enhancing economic development in Africa (Al-Roubaie 2010) and in demonstrating the philosophical thinking of the Africans (Ramose 1999; Shutte 2001).

Yet as already alluded to, the truth remains that in Africa, like elsewhere, IKSs were used to administer peace, harmony, and order amongst the people and their physical and spiritual environment. There is need to emphasise the moral import of IKSs in promoting peace, harmony and order in the African traditional society. This scenario changed with the advent of colonialism in Africa which marginalised and demonised IKSs leaving their potentials for establishing and maintaining a moral, virtuous society, shattered and never exploited any further. It is in this light that this chapter argues for a correction to the vestiges of colonialism, neo-colonialism, and the western gaze that demonised African IKSs and posed fatal challenges to their [IKSs] potentials in improving African societies socially, economically, and morally. While the chapter generally focuses on IKSs vis-a-vis morality in Africa, it adopts Zimbabwe and Mozambique as case studies in showing the beauty of the undiluted African indigenous knowledge systems and their potential for establishing a moral, virtuous society. To this end, the chapter makes the argument that Africa, today, is in the grips of high crime rates, serious moral decadence, and other social calamities because of the marginalisation, false, and pejorative label attached to the African IKSs. In view of this argument, the chapter goes further to criticise, dismantle, and challenge the inherited colonial legacies, which have socially and morally injured many African societies.

Background to Africa's IKSs vis-a-vis moral life

The socio-political and cultural dimensions of the Western hegemonic tendencies in the world's global affairs have posed serious challenges, especially to its former African colonies. The West considered Africa as a 'dark continent', and hence despised its traditions, customs, belief systems, and indigenous knowledge systems as diabolic, barbaric, and backward. This had a negative impact on Africa's own socio-economic and political development. Africa's valued traditions and knowledge systems had to change to fit in with the western scientism and modernity. A selected number of African indigenous knowledge systems will be analysed with a view to providing a more rounded and objective view of the African continent. In doing this, the chapter adopts Zimbabwe and Mozambique as case studies. It clearly reiterates that 'Europe's intervention in Africa [was] the beginning of the most nefarious images. An African invention, for European purposes, could no longer serve the interests of its own people' (Asante in Mengara 2001), as Europeans despised all African traditions, customs, and knowledge systems. In view of this, the chapter seeks to rekindle and explicates the African philosophy debate as an African response to demonization inherent in the western discourses on Africa. It is a rationality debate, a deconstructionist effort reminiscent of the many aspects of the African people's struggles to control their own identity, society, and destination. How African indigenous knowledge systems, particularly some selected IKSs from the people of Mozambique and Zimbabwe, are critical in the establishment and propagation of a moral, virtuous society will be examined. In the cultures of these two countries are distinguished IKSs that in the past were used as the precepts and codes of conduct that harmonised the people of one society with that of the other. The cultures of these two countries share a lot in common in terms of traditions, customs, beliefs, and knowledge systems due to their common origin as Bantu and also through intermarriages.

More importantly, despite the cultural onslaught on African thought, particularly their knowledge and belief systems through the spread of the western scientific worldview and the Christian religious tradition, the Mozambicans and Zimbabweans never completely lost touch with their traditional thought and values. The traditional belief system has continued to inform much of the life and activities of the people of these two societies. Their common beliefs in traditions of avenging spirits (*ngozi*); fencing a wife/husband using a charm (*runyoka*); fencing property using a charm/anti-theft charm (*rukwa/muzazata*); communal proverbs (*tsumo*); folktales (*ngano*); and taboos (*zvierwa*) are still critical in maintaining a moral, virtuous society, especially in the country sides where traditions are still seriously observed. In this light, the chapter calls for a return of Africa to its traditions and knowledge systems. This is what Amilcar Cabral (1974) and Masolo (1995) (together with Aime Cesaire, 2001) respectively call a 'return to the source' and the call for a 'return to the native land' – one of the many revolutionary expressions of the then rising black militantism, nationalism, and Africanism [...] to counter Westernism's arrogant and aggressive Eurocentric culture. I argue with Nigel Gibson (2011: 52) here that such a return requires a 'mental liberation from all the inferiority complexes that had been produced from years of living in apartheid South Africa'. This return is necessary for Zimbabwe and Mozambique, and by extension the rest of Africa, to reverse poverty and destitution which revolutionalists cum theorists like Biko (1978: 52) believed were 'not endemic to Africa but a product of colonialism and apartheid'.

In the light of the above, a return for Africans to their indigenous knowledge systems such as *rukwa, ngozi, runyoka, tsumo, ngano,* and *zvierwa* could be a better survival strategy for the cultures of the two societies (Mozambique and Zimbabwe) and by extension Africa, if 'real peace' and a moral virtuous society are to be successfully established. From this survival strategy, Christine Obbo's (2006) observation is apt: 'As ever, power is key to ownership of the knowledge production process. Contemporary problems of development, health, and indigenous knowledge demand that we define the theoretical agendas and practical issues that are of concern to us'. Thus, rather than being passive assimilators of European modernity, Africans should take an active role in the selection and, at times, fusion of what they got from Europe and what they already had as a people. This surviving strategy is failing in many African societies due to the impact of Western scientism and modernity – forces that despise African traditions and knowledge systems as diabolic, backward, and superstitious. It is argued for the fusion of the already existing Euro-specific modernity-tradition ideology in Africa with African modernity. Ngugi wa Thiongo (1981) sees the fruition of this possibility, only if the liberation of natural and human resources and the entire production forces of the nation, would be the beginning of Africa's real progress and development.

What indigenous knowledge system is and is not?

Since time immemorial Indigenous Knowledge Systems (IKSs) were used by societies in Africa and the rest of the world for various purposes depending on the needs of the society in question. IKSs, thus, have survived for a very long time. But, what are IKSs? The *http://www.sedac.ciesin.columbia.edu* website defines IKS as 'local knowledge that is unique to a given culture or society'. They are knowledge forms that have failed to die despite the racial and colonial onslaughts that they have suffered at the hands of Western imperialism and arrogance. These 'forms of knowledge, referred to as IKSs, have originated locally and naturally' (Altieri, 1995).

Considering the sense of these two definitions, I identify with Ocholla (2007) who defines IKSs as 'a complex set of knowledge and technologies existing and developed around specific conditions of populations and communities indigenous to a particular geographic location. These complex sets of knowledge and technologies are developed through the processes of acculturation and through kinship relationships that societal groups form, and are handed down to the posterity through oral tradition and cultural practices such as rituals and rites. As such, IKSs are the adhesives that bind society as they constitute communicative processes through which knowledge is transmitted, preserved, and acquired by humans in their different societies. Yet, as has been explained by Ocholla (2007: 3) IKSs have over the years been:

> illegitimated, illegalised, suppressed and abandoned by some communities, and the countries and peoples practicing it were condemned and associated with outdatedness, a characteristic most people find demeaning. This form of marginalisation produced a generation that for the most, does not understand, recognise, appreciate, value or use IK. Arguably, this situation has produced an intellectually colonised mindset.

Put aside Ocholla's observations above, it is worth noting that because *ngozi, runyoka, rukwa, tsumo, ngano,* and *zvierwa* – IKs discussed in this chapter – are transmitted through cultural rites (for example, rituals) through socialisation processes and can be appropriated through kinship ties, they qualify to be coined an indigenous knowledge system. The aforementioned IKSs are a commonplace in Zimbabwe and Mozambique, especially among the Shona ethnic groups. According to Ermine (cited in Hammersmith 2007), 'it can be elaborated that IKSs are linked to the communities that produce them'. He further observed that, 'those natural communities are characterised by complex kinship systems of relationships among people, animals, the earth, and the cosmos from which knowing emanates' (cited in Hammersmith 2007). These knowledge forms are known by other names, and among them are indigenous ways of knowing, traditional knowledge, indigenous technical knowledge, and rural knowledge as well as ethno-science (Altieri 1995) or people's science. Indigenous knowledge systems manifest themselves through different dimensions. Among these are agriculture, medicine, security, botany, zoology, craft skills and linguistics. In matters relating to security, especially of properties like homes, field crops and livestock, the indigenous people developed some mechanisms that are still used in some rural areas to safeguard their properties from thieves and invaders (e.g. hexing). They have also developed traditional ways of weather forecasting that helped them to plan their activities for at least two to three days in advance. This knowledge was very useful, especially in summer and immediately after harvesting when crops, like finger millet, would be in need of thrashing and winnowing. Indigenous ways of knowing have also brought forth useful knowledge on medicine and health. The use of, for example, proverbs and idioms is another case of ethno-knowledge that has been used in both judicial and governance matters.

It is curious to note that IKSs as those forms of knowledge that the people of the formerly colonised countries survived on before the advent of colonialism were swept aside and denigrated by the colonialists and their sciences as backward and superstitious. This was chiefly because the colonialists sought to give themselves some form of justification on why they had to colonise other people's lands. As they occupied these countries, they did not only subject the indigenes to inhuman treatment, but they also took away their lands and renamed them using names from the metropolis, and added insult to injury by claiming that the indigenes were in the dark and were backward. This is exemplified through the works of 'scholars such as David Hume, Immanuel Kant, and Hegel who surprisingly denied reason, the most essential quality of humanity, to other groups of people' (Winch 1970) like Africans. It is surprising that America subsequently joined the Western imperial tune of looking down upon people of other societies having itself suffered the same labelling as that of Africa. Paracelsus, the sixteenth century European medical writer, for example, pictured North America as a continent peopled with creatures that were half human, half beast. The Bishop of Santa Marta in Colombia, South America, likewise described the local Indians as 'not men with rational souls but wild men of the woods, for which reason they could retain no Christian doctrine, no virtue nor any kind of learning' (Pagden 1982: 23).

The nexus between African indigenous knowledge systems and African cosmology

Fundamentally, the African traditional customs and practices emphasise the close connections between the empirical world and the cosmos. Parallels can be drawn between the consequences of good and bad, given that the cosmological world (*vadzimu* and *musikavanhu*) (ancestors and God/ the creator, respectively) govern the empirical world, and in consequence, judges humanity according to the virtue of their deeds. Gonese (1999) observes that the cosmovision of the Shona people is based on three worlds: the human world, the spiritual world, and the natural world. He further suggests that spirit mediums act as intermediaries between mortal beings and the living dead or ancestral spirits. Transcending Gonese's view, I argue that indigenous knowledge systems are the adhesive vice grips that bind spirit mediums, rain petitioners, and rural dwellers' social relations together by setting the ground rules, in terms of cultural practices and customs observance in their communities. These knowledge systems are used, for example, in the processions of rain making ceremonies, witch-naming ceremonies, and ceremonies for appeasing the dead. In light of the coordination or facilitation roles in spiritual activities that IKSs perform, the latter should be conceived as a spiritual commitment of the 'land dwellers' to the ancestors of the land through allegiance to the traditions, values, and customs known through the knowledge systems. Even new comers should be introduced to both the society's indigenous knowledge systems and the ancestors of the land that are believed to protect the inhabitants of that land. This is often affected through the process of *kusuma*[1], which involves elders of the land pouring beer onto the ground and making meditations on connecting the new comer to the ancestors for spiritual protection and material growth.

It is curious to note that in the Shona traditional societies the IKSs were, for a long time, used to perpetuate a moral, virtuous society, among other reasons. The IKSs were multifunctional, depending on the demands and needs of the society; hence the same systems can still be employed for the same reasons/motivations, even today. This supports Meki Nzewi's (2007) position that 'contemporary Africans must strive to rescue, resuscitate, and advance our original intellectual legacy or the onslaught of externally manipulated forces of mental and cultural dissociation now rampaging Africa will obliterate our original intellect and lore of life'. This is important because what is distinctively "African" in morality as in metaphysics in Africa today and by extrapolation among the Shona derives from African traditional thought and needs. Nzewi (2007) continues his argument through Touma by saying: If our ancestors had no sound intellectual mettle, how did they develop the scientific cultures of food, childbirth, and mental nurture, also the musical arts genres that were non sanctionable mediators in the indigenous societal polity and social-cultural practices, including the policing of egalitarian law and order, medical arts delivery, etc.? To the Africans in general and in particular the Shona, the concept of IKSs is central not only to their metaphysics, but to their moral being. IKSs, however, has been despised and their credence suffered tremendously in the face of modernity, logical positivism, and/or scientisation.

---

[1] *Kusuma* means introduction to the higher authority like ancestral spirits.

The providence of science in explaining phenomena, owes itself to its internal logic, perceived objectivity, and power of prediction that may not immediately apply to metaphysical beliefs of IKSs such as *ngozi, rukwa, runyoka, tsumo, ngano* and *zvierwa*. As Harding (1994) suggests, most of the greatest successes of science owe to its 'internal logic' be it as inductivism, crucial experiments, the hypothetico-deductive method, or a cycle of normal science-revolution-normal science. I infer from Harding that the authority of science rest upon its objective claims and its ability to render scientific proof that is perceivably immune to personal biases, preferences, and values. Given the complexity of establishing scientific proof about the moral value and even existence of IKSs, it is surprising how the subject of IKSs has not attracted the much needed curiosity amongst scientists, but rather left to anthropologists, sociologists, and philosophers. A complementary view is that IKSs rest on internalism and, as such, cannot be subjected to scientific rigor. As Ikuenobe (2000) suggests, internalism suggests that rationality is a function of the properties of beliefs, such as coherence, to which one has internal access. The belief in IKS, such as *ngozi, rukwa, runyoka,* and *zvierwa*, is internalist in orientation – it invokes some internally coherent claims about an explanation of the functioning of the cosmology to which scientific investigation is less privileged to infer from or draw on. IKSs' functioning defies recourse to scientific explanation or prediction to sufficiently substantiate its existence and more importantly its moral relevance. Yet the challenge is that the authority of science and its hegemonic influence on epistemology and knowledge production has undermined possibilities for other epistemological alternatives for explicating social reality or nature in ways that fall outside the frameworks of science. Particularly how IKSs can illuminate our knowledge of cosmology and what new insights about indigenous knowledge systems could be gained from exploration of this reality. The dominance of science and perceptions about its opaqueness to the public have 'led to a focus on 'back-end' consequences such as risk, in effect protecting the broader trajectory of scientific and technological development from accountability' (Davies, McCallie, Simonsson, Lehr & Duensing 2009). This raises critical questions about whether different forms of knowledge cannot be developed outside the terms and parameters defined by science. What is lost in the process of moving from conventional scientific inquiry towards the unorthodox processes of searching for other forms of knowing? These questions cannot be adequately addressed without challenging the monopoly of science as the predominant way of accessing, communicating, and transmitting knowledge. The rise in 'citizen science', participatory processes of public understanding and even challenging of science research is the direct consequence of public frustration with the limitations of science.

My work cannot, necessarily, be conceived as citizen science, but rather seeks to contribute to the IKSs debate by arguing that IKSs, such as *ngozi, rukwa, runyoka, tsumo, ngano* and *zvierwa*, constitute indigenous knowledge systems that could contribute to easing the tapestry of African continent's human development. That is to say, these IKSs embody a hidden genre of 'moral epistemology' or different form of knowledge that could contribute, in multiple ways, to resolving Africa's development dilemmas, if it cast in the open for debate, and integrated into mainstream expert science. I argue that the exploration of IKSs is a potentially productive indigenous knowledge system that, for a long time, has been conceived as diabolic by Western civilisation and whose developmental essence remains shrouded in mystery.

Zimbabwean and Mozambican case studies of morally informed IKSs

While IKSs are a common feature in Mozambican and Zimbabwean traditional societies and, by extension, Africa and beyond, this chapter makes reference to the Shona people of Mozambique and Zimbabwe. This selection has been made possible by the fact that the researcher is conversant with the Shona culture in both countries, Mozambique and Zimbabwe.

The term, 'Shona' refers to various linguistic dialect groups who occupy the greater part of Zimbabwe and central western part of Mozambique (see Mawere 2010). In Zimbabwe, the Shona constitute one of the largest communal-cultural groups (Gelfand 1973). The distinction in the dialects was made more prominent and pronounced by the early missionaries and settlers working in different parts of the country, which is the reason why Ranger (1985) argues that these language differences are actually a colonial invention. Although in different geographical locations there is so much horizontal similarity across the spectrum of the small ethnic groups that are classified as the Shona in both Mozambique and Zimbabwe as they share a common language. In Mozambique, a number of dialect groups are generally referred to as Shona, but under the armpit of the dialect Ndau. These include the Dondo in the districts of Dondo and Beira in Sofala province; the Danda in the districts of Chibabava (Sofala) and Machaze in the Manica province; the Vauteve in the district of Chimoo in the Manica providence; and the Manyika, who occupy the largest part of Manica province (Mawere 2010).

It is worth noting that there is so much horizontal similarity across the spectrum of the small ethnic groups (in both Mozambique and Zimbabwe) that are classified as the Shona as they share a common culture, language, and philosophy of life. As pointed out by Ranger (1985), prior to the development of written Shona dialects, there was a situation in which this whole group spoke a single, common language. Although now found in different geographical locations, there is ample evidence that the Shona of Mozambique and Zimbabwe still 'share most of their cultural beliefs, language, and philosophies of life' (Mawere 2010: 272). The belief in indigenous knowledge systems such as avenging spirit (*ngozi*), fencing a wife (*runyoka*), fencing property (*rukwa*), proverbs (*tsumo*), folktale (*ngano*), and taboos (*zvierwa*) is still commonplace across the whole spectrum of the Shona culture.

Though suffering criticism from empirical scientists, it remains a truism for the Shona traditionalists that IKSs can be used to institute and foster a virtuous, moral society. In the Shona society and by extension Africa in general, this is possible because the violation of systems such as *ngozi, rukwa, runyoka, tsumo, ngano,* and *zvierwa* results in 'natural justice', taking its own course against the perpetrator. In fact, the offender (sometimes together with his/her family) faces fatal consequences. This chapter seeks to show how indigenous knowledge systems such as *ngozi, rukwa, runyoka, tsumo, ngano,* and *zvierwa* were used as 'theories of justice' to institute and promote a virtuous, moral society. The study further proposes that these indigenous knowledge systems can still be used as 'theories of justice' for the same purpose in modern-day Mozambique, Zimbabwe, Africa and beyond, if we are to establish a morally virtuous society. This, however, is only possible if the richness of the continent in terms of IKs that are uniquely African is shown in full flower without bias and any further marginalisation or subjugation.

Nurturing a moral, virtuous society: IKSs' roles in influencing and promoting good moral behaviour

♦ *Zvier[w]a (Taboos)*

Although some indigenous knowledge systems still prevail in Africa, most of these systems have failed to stand the test of time. Others are gravitating towards extinction. This has been due to the Western scientism and modernity. Western hegemonic tendencies have demonised African indigenous knowledge systems and advanced the view that they were diabolic, barbaric, and backward. One of the indigenous knowledge systems that have suffered these unfortunate changes is taboos (*zvier[w]a*). *Zvierwa*, which are also known as "the inviolable" or "the sacred" (Pearsall 1999; Mawere and Kadenge 2010), were a common tradition in Mozambique and Zimbabwe and remain a legitimate system of the everyday lives of traditionalists and custodians of the Shona culture in these countries today. Taboos include both 'real taboos' and 'false taboos' (Mawere & Kadenge, 2010: 31). False taboos are 'those which are only meant to keep check on children' (Mawere and Kadenge 2010: 33). These taboos are only particular to children and not universal, as adults know that they are not real. *Usagara munzira unozoita mamota* (do not sit in the path, you will suffer from boils) and *usafuridza mubhodhoro amai vako vanozopindamo vakatadza kubuda* (do not blow into a bottle, your mother will enter into it and will fail to come out) are typical examples of false taboos. These taboos are false because their violation does not result in the said consequences.

On the other hand, 'real taboos are those which, when violated by any person, young or old, the offender/violator and his/her family suffered serious consequences' (Mawere and Kadenge 2010: 31). Real taboos, thus, are not meant to cast fear in children or anyone by using empty threats. However, real consequences can be observed, both by children and elders, who violate them. For example, taboos such as *usarara nemusikana/mukadzi ari kutevera kana kuti arikumwedzi unorwara* (do not have sex with a menstruating woman as this may result in the illness of the male partner) and *usatuka, kurova kana kuuraya amai vako, unotanda botso* (do not scold, beat, or kill your mother as this would result in you suffering from botso, an avenging spirit of your own mother/societal denial if the

100

mother is still alive) are real taboos. It is unfortunate that the Shona elders and scholars could not explain the causal relationship between the real taboos and their consequences, which is largely metaphysical and not scientific in nature. This failure has led to the undermining of taboos and, consequently, to their phasing out, especially in the face of empirical science/scientism. Yet, it remains a truism that violation of any of the real taboos in the Shona culture will result in fatal ramifications to the perpetrator. Violation of the real taboo, *usarara nemusikana/mukadzi ari kutevera kana kuti arikumwedzi unorwara*, for instance, would result in the perpetrator(s) contracting sexually transmitted diseases (STDs).

In the light of this observation, I contend that taboos are 'ethical codes of conduct/commandments', just like the Biblical commandments and the Hippocratic Oath that guided Christians and physicians, respectively, since time immemorial. They (taboos) are commandments/codes of conduct used by the Shona, especially before the advent of the Bible with its commandments. From this understanding, I argue that taboos, especially the 'real taboos', should be reinstituted as this can help establishing a virtuous, moral society; a society characterised with peaceful, morally responsible, and caring members who can respect their environment and other community members. Taboos, of course together with the Bible, can indeed impact positively on people's behaviour and in peace building among the Shona, Africa, and beyond. Taboos, thus, constitute as an African ethno-science /technology (body of ethno-scientific knowledge) that can be used to establish a morally virtuous society.

◆ *Runyoka (Fencing a woman/man using charm)*

The conceptualisation of *runyoka*, also known as 'fidelity charm' or 'fencing a woman or man with charm', is marred with controversies of epic proportions to the extent that pinning down a precise definition of the concept is not any easy thing. According to the International Conference on ADIS (1993), about 30% of the traditional healers interviewed said *runyoka* and AIDS were similar, while 68% claimed they could provide treatment for *runyoka*. Most of the healers regarded *runyoka* as a weapon used to punish people who committed adultery, while some more said it was a way of determining whether a wife or husband was faithful. According to the same report, some members of the public considered *runyoka* as a form of witchcraft while others understood it as a method used by some people to punish enemies through their wives. This view resonates with the Shona people's [of Zimbabwe] adage: *mukadzi wemumwe ndiambuya* (Another person's wife is just like your mother-in-law). Almost all the traditional healers interviewed claimed medical doctors could not cure *runyoka* because it involved witchcraft and required an herbalistic approach. Healers also felt that doctors should take traditional healers seriously and give them a chance to look at the AIDS patients. Since violation of *runyoka* results in a mysterious disease, I define *runyoka* as a complex venereal disease caused by sleeping with a fenced (using herbs/charm) woman or man. The fencing can be done by either partner to ensure that the spouse would not be involved in prostitution or adulterous activities. In a report given in the Herald (2010), for example:

> Seremwa, a native of Gambura village in Chinhoyi district recently died in mysterious circumstances after complaining of severe stomach pains and later acting like a fish before spending two nights in a bathtub filled with water. She would intermittently gulp the water and then spew it out like a fish. Hospital medical superintendent, Dr. Collett Mawire, confirmed the strange incident. A woman who saw Seremwa when she was at the hospital said, Seremwa was complaining of suffering from extreme heat and dehydration whenever she got out of the water and

had confessed to being intimate with a man who had been 'fixed/fenced' by his wife. The practice is known as runyoka or 'fencing' in many circles. She would say the man's mother had warned her not to hang around the man indicating that he had been fixed with runyoka by his wife. She regretted not listening to the man's mother.

In another incident, it is revealed by the Doktorsnake website, *http://en.wikipedia.org/wiki/Africa*, that the Mount Darwin secretary for the Zimbabwe National Traditional Healers' Association, Benson Kaseke said the following of *runyoka*:

> Although runyoka is not approved by traditional healers, it is widespread in the Mukumbura area of Mount Darwin, on the border of Mozambique. Runyoka is typically used by people who suspect their spouses of playing away from home as no one wants to live with an unfaithful partner, hence the need for runyoka. Kaseke further explains that in some cases, daughters are given runyoka by their parents so that they cannot engage in premarital sex.

As can be seen, *runyoka* is a 'safety lock' applied on both men and women to enforce fidelity. A series of tantalising and baffling questions which necessitate serious investigation, however, arise: "To what extent are claims and cases of *runyoka* among the Shona people justify the need for revival of this cultural heritage? To what extent could *runyoka* provide a safety net as well as checks and balance in relation to adultery, prostitution and HIV/Aids epidemic in Zimbabwe, Mozambique and beyond?" Similar questions could be raised in view of the issue of *rukwa* discussed below.

Yet, because the practice of *runyoka* is linked to witchcraft, it may result to death of the perpetrator(s). It is, nowadays, despised in the Shona and other African societies. It can, however, be argued that distortions and misconceptions about *runyoka* arise from the 'pollution' of traditional African culture by colonialism. Thus, it remains a fact that *runyoka* enforces fidelity between spouses and can be used to establish a virtuous, moral society which might also be free from sexually transmitted diseases and HIV/AIDS pandemic. The reason that the Zimbabweans and Mozambicans, as a result of Western influences, are shunning the use of *runyoka* contributes to the ever-increasing number of people committing adultery and others contracting HIV/AIDS. It is the contentions of this work that if IKSs, such as *runyoka*, are continually used in the Shona societies, Africa and beyond, this would help to establish a morally virtuous society; a society free of immorally sexual beings and HIV/AIDS.

◆ *Rukwa (Fencing property using charm)*

Though a common practice among the Shona people, especially in the countryside, there is a scarce recorded literature on fencing property using charming/property fencing charm (*rukwa*). This is perhaps because the practice is closely associated with witchcraft though also used to deter potential rapists, adulterers and even prostitutes. Among the Shona themselves, the Ndau people (an ethnic group under the umbrella Shona) of both Zimbabwe and Mozambique are well known for the use of *rukwa* in safeguarding or protecting their property from thieves and 'invaders'. In this light, I define *rukwa* as medicine or a charm used to safeguard property: it is fencing (using a charm) property from thieves and invaders. In an interview the researcher held in Manica Province, Mozambique (2010), the traditional healer, Sekuru Gogoyo, revealed that:

> Rukwa is used to safeguard one's property by mysteriously catching the thief and preventing him/her

from escaping until the owner arrives. One of the most common methods of administering rukwa is the use of a small bottle. One would secretly put some traditional herbs (given by a traditional healer) in the small bottle, close the bottle, and dump it at the doorstep of his/her bedroom, shop, or field (where he or she wants to protect the property). The magic charm would catch any thief that dares coming in to steal away the property.

The *rukwa* charm, thus, is supposed to safeguard and prevent the property in the house, shop, field, or any other place where the property is kept. Any thief or invader that dares coming in to steal away the property risks the humiliation of being caught in the act by the owner, as s/he would be unable to leave the premise because of the power of the magic charm. "The thief can only be freed when the owner comes, summons the community to witness the event, and then strikes the thief two to three times using a whip" added Sekuru Gogoyo (2010).

Although some people, due to Western influence, links *rukwa* to witchcraft, I argue that to understand the logic of *rukwa* fully, one has to seek its meaning and moral relevance in the culture where it is a function. As such, *rukwa*, as with *runyoka*, is a 'safety lock' applied by the Shonas on thieves to cultivate in them good behaviour or respect of other people's property. *Rukwa* tames thieves into fully responsible citizens by deterring them from tampering with or stealing other people's property. In the light of this understanding, I contend that IKSs such as *rukwa*, should continue to be used in the Shona societies, Africa, and beyond if a morally virtuous 'society' is to be established. *Rukwa* continues to be a good 'moral teacher' for the thieves and potential thieves.

♦ *Ngozi (Avenging Spirit)*

Technically, *ngozi* is the spirit of a person who has been murdered and then comes back to seek revenge in the family of the murderer by causing unfathomable sorrow through illnesses, misfortunes, or a series of deaths until the perpetrator pays reparations to the offended family (Mawere 2005). In fact, *ngozi* can be understood as an *African theory of justice* with an equivalence of theories of justices by Western scholars such as John Rawls. As a theory of justice, *ngozi* is premised on the ideas of 'teat for tat' and fairness.

In the Shona culture, when the guilty family has failed, deliberately or otherwise, to pay restitution, strikes viciously and harshly by not only targeting the perpetrator of the crime, but his kinsmen as well. As Bourdillon (1976) remarks, '*ngozi* is fearsome and terrifying because it attacks suddenly and very harshly'. *Ngozi* will only stop causing harm and death in the family of the murderer/perpetrator after it is appeased (Mawere 2005). It is important to note that, among the Shona people, it is not always the case that the wrongdoer is the one who gets killed or cursed by *ngozi*, but any person who is a blood relative of the wrongdoer is subject to the anger of *ngozi*. The victim of the murder needs to be replaced by compensation in the form of a herd of cattle and a virgin girl, if the murdered person was a man, and a herd of cattle and a small boy, if the murdered person was a woman. The guilty family, thus, is given the option to either pay reparation or suffers the consequences through wreaking havoc, for example, causing a series of misfortunes, deaths, and illnesses. In a recent interview with The Standard (2010), Vimbai Chivaura, a lecturer at the University of Zimbabwe, considers *ngozi* as a crime. He thus says:

Haven't you heard people say, usatiparire ngozi? Ngozi imhosva inoda kuripwa (Ngozi is a crime that demands restitution). Prime ngozi arise when innocent blood is shed.

If you kill a person, you will have terminated all the plans for that person. Even if no one knows that you have done so, you have to acknowledge the crime and pay reparations. When human beings die, their souls would be separated from their body. That soul will torment those who committed the crimes.

As is revealed in his comment, and indeed so, restitution partly constitutes the Shona/African justice system. Usually, life lost is replenished with life. That is why a young girl or boy is usually given to the offended family in marriage in order to continue the life of the deceased through her or his off-springs. This way the cosmological balance disturbed by the outrageous act of murder is restored. This is so because the Shonas are essentially spiritual people in a general outlook. Their conception of justice is very different from the Westerners'. As previously highlighted, to the Shona people, *ngozi* is an integral part of their justice system. For the Shona, human life, thus, is one of the most valuable assets in the Shona society and *ngozi* is essentially an expression of disapproval when it comes to actions that result in taking away life. Hence, to the Shona people, *ngozi* (manslaughter understood in terms of the dire circumstances that follow failure to atone) has a regulatory function which is that of deterrence, rather than retribution.

Due to these atrocities caused by *ngozi*, the threat posed by the latter is feared by everyone in the Shona culture. It is this fear that, for a long time, has maintained harmony among the Shonas and has made them peace-loving people. In view of this observation, I contend that the Shona societies and Africa should continue employing *ngozi* to deter potential murderers in their societies. Resultantly, this would lead to the establishment of a virtuous, moral society; a society with people who respect others' lives.

♦ *Ngano (Folk tales)*

As noted by Kothari (2007: 4), 'some forms of traditional knowledge are expressed through stories, legends, folklore, rituals, songs, art, and even laws', of which *ngano* (folk tale) is one example. Folk tales are stories, but not mere stories. I have pointed out in one of my works Mawere (2013: 8) that, folk tales are:

> Stories that mature people recount to young children especially those undergoing elementary education, but even adult persons could also listen to the stories. The stories, which are told by a story teller, are often fictitious but generated to offer a wide range of lessons to the young children and serve to inculcate values in them.

Though now no longer told in many African societies due to Westernisation, *ngano* (in Shona of Zimbabwe – both singular and plural) were told at night during dry season. This was understood to be the ideal time for telling the stories so as not to interrupt normal activities of the day. The stories which involved different characters such as animals, human beings, birds and snakes were often thrilling but full of didactic lessons for the audience to pick up. In the stories, villains were often punished and good characters rewarded as a way of teaching the young to shun bad behaviour. In fact, *ngano* could be understood as part of the African traditional curriculum. It is in this light that I argue that *ngano* is one form of [African] indigenous knowledge system that has always been used to nurture and promote a moral, harmonious, peaceful society especially prior to colonialism and Westernisation of African societies.

Concluding remarks

This chapter has unravelled the concept of indigenous knowledge systems, particularly *zvierwa, rukwa, runyoka, tsumo, ngano,* and *ngozi,* exposing the different dimensions that it has assumed as it was constructed and evolved over the years in rural Mozambique and Zimbabwe. I have emphasised the need for the reversal of the Euro-centric paradigms of Africa, where the perjured interpretations of African IKSs have remained grafted on the mental processes and human aspirations of modern Africans, thereby robbing them of their intellectual confidence, mental identity, and socio-economic development across the continent. Although colonialism has intimidated and made attempts to conquer the African mind, it is my fervent hope, in the words of Nzewi (2007), that 'after the bombardment of the invading tornados of fanciful knowledge, the indigenous lore of life will yet revive with innately refurbished shoots, and fulfil again the human mission of the musical arts in original Africa, and edify Africa's mental and human posterity'.

The present study, thus, has tried to give critical insights in showing that the negative images of IKSs should not remain forever on the 'map'. The chapter has shown that the time is now that African people's worldview should assume a place as a global power through African organised cultural systems. We are faced with new challenges that have literally taken the continent by storm, what Nzewi (2007) has called 'the supersonic wizardry', which is an imperial encirclement and mental enslavement 'from which the images of the Africans are marked absent, except in negativity, a retreat into the culture and, thus, an Afrocentric worldview is mandatory' (Springer 2003). It is this African spirituality that is inseparable from African philosophy, which continues to pervade, guide, illuminate, and empower Africans' existence into the unborn tomorrows with renewed vigour (Springer 2003).

More importantly, the chapter has argued that IKSs have a potential to boost moral probity among the Shonas and, by extension, Africans. They constitute a foundation for the establishment of a morally virtuous society. It should be recommended, however, that collaborative efforts by the governments of Mozambique and Zimbabwe, traditional institutions and civil society could cultivate civil education against the abuse of IKSs. As the study has demonstrated, violation of IKSs brings 'natural justice' against the perpetrator(s). In this light, the chapter has suggested that re-institution of IKSs and the reversal of the Euro-centric paradigms of Africa are critical in restoring the Africans' consciousness and establishing a morally virtuous society.

Chapter 5

Africa and the search for an African framework for development

Introduction

Africa is one continent that is richly endowed with resources of all kinds — minerals, forests, fishery, animals, birds, water, sunshine and many others. It is also a continent with many multi-talented experts. Contrary to this reality, Africa is ranked one of the poorest continents in the world. The immediate question that comes to mind is: If Africa a continent rich in resources and raw materials why then ranked one of the poorest in the world? A similar question can be raised against the second observation that if Africa has highly educated and multi-talented people why then does it lags behind other continents?

The aforementioned questions necessitate research on Africa on issues of economic development. While the questions raised above are too complex to be answered in a word as there are many factors that affect development in Africa, there is no doubt that slavery, colonialism and some exploitative multi-national companies have played an important role in under-developing Africa. In fact, since the beginning of slavery, Africa has always been short-changed or cheated by the outside world especially the western world. Since this chapter focuses mainly on development, most of the examples I will give in this chapter are in line with issues of economic development.

How the West and America have terrorised and underdeveloped Africa over the years?

There is too much talk about Africa, particularly on why the continent of Africa remains one of the poorest in the world when in fact, it is one of the richest continents resource-wise. While I acknowledge that the answer to that question is too complex to answer in a word, I believe there are compound factors that explain the poverty trends in Africa. Below, I explain some of the factors that try to explain the African situation. But before that it should be noted that the aforementioned factors, emanate from the three basic historical epochs identifiable in the history of the African continent namely, the pre-colonial period; the colonial period, and the post-colonial period. The first epoch, as Ogundele (2006: 697) notes, refers to the era before the advent of Arabs who represented Islam, and Europeans as well as Americans who represented Christianity. The two religions (Christianity and Islam) are significant for the African continent's disunity, disharmony and destabilisation. They were both associated with the Slave Trade, colonialism, and post-colonialism. The second epoch is the Slave Trade/colonial era characterised with the invasion, conquest and subjugation of African cultures (Mawere 2014), while the third epoch is the post-colonial/neo-colonial era, which, just like its colonial predecessor, is driven by both foreigners and the African ruling elite. In the ensuing paragraphs, I elaborate on the factors that explain Africa's situation.

Racial slavery

Racial slavery as an extreme form of inequality in which some individuals of one race are literally owned by others of another race as their property has had a lasting impact on Africa: it dehumanised, impoverished and underdeveloped the African people. It is a known historical fact that European

112

imperial countries merchandised young and able-bodied Africans such that Africa lost many of its sons and daughters to Europe and subsequently to United States of America during slave trade. In fact, 'starting in the sixteen century *till 1888 when slavery was finally abolished*, about ten *to fifteen* million blacks were transported to the American continent as slaves: some two million in the seventeenth century; in the eighteenth century, about six million; and roughly two million in the nineteenth century' (Giddens 1993: 261; emphasis original). At the same time, about four million Africans were transported to Brazil to work in the plantations. In Angola alone, the African country that paid the heaviest price in terms of losing her sons and daughters as slaves to the West, 'in three hundred years four million Angolans were unloaded from the slave ships on to the shores of the Americas. To this recorded number, must be added the proportion that were shipwrecked or died during the crossing – in some cases as many as 80 per cent' (Humbaraci and Nicole, 1974: 88). The European imperialists achieved this mainly through the institution of systematic terrorism and many other forms of violence that forced the [African] victims to relinquish their sovereignties and dignities (both individual and collective) and helplessly surrendered themselves as commodities to be exploited economically or otherwise. Some [slaves] died along their way to Europe. As Henry Nevinson (1906: 113) writes,

> The path is strewn with dead men's [and women's] bones. You see the white thighbones lying in front of your feet, and at one side, among the undergrowth, you find the skull. These are the skeletons of slaves who have been unable to keep up with the march, and so were murdered or left to die.

The experience of slaves (and slavery as a system) is best described by Toyin Falola thus:

The experience of slavery was one of human suffering that is hard to describe. The wars that produced the captives sold into slavery were traumatizing. Then came the Middle Passage—when the slaves were transported across the sea. Stripped, dehumanized, and branded, they were packed into small spaces and fed contaminated food and water. Dysentery, smallpox, and measles were among the diseases that afflicted a huge number. Many did not make it—one out of six never survived the journey. Those who made it arrived 'looking like skeletons' ... [T]hey were 'completely naked, and are shut up in a large court or enclosure . . . for as a rule are left to lie on the ground, naked without shelter.' Buyers examined and auctioned them like cattle. Then came the experience on the plantations where they were treated as property, regarded as no better than cattle (Falola 2002: 116).

Joseph Miller also offers a similarly detailed description of the salve experience. Miller (2002: 49, emphasis original), thus, records:

The great majority of the slaves went directly to the slave pens ... These barracoons – a word also applied to farmyards for keeping animals—were usually barren enclosures. Large numbers of slaves accumulated within these pens, living for days and weeks surrounded by walls too high for a person to scale, squatting helplessly, naked, on the dirt and entirely exposed to the skies except for a few adjoining cells where they could be locked at night. They lived in a 'wormy morass' ... and slept in their own excrement, without even a bonfire for warmth ..., and realising the cruelty of Europeans, the enslaved were Africans physically and psychologically tormented only by seeing them: All slaves trembled in terror at meeting the white cannibals of the cities, the first Europeans whom many of the slaves would have seen. They feared the whites' intention of converting African brains' into cheese or rendering the fat of African bodies into cooking oil, as well as burning their bones into gunpowder.

As such, most of the slaves were deprived of almost all their rights as human beings in law, in the false labelling or stereotyping that they were inferior to the white race. This was meant to establish an exploitative relationship as the slave trade could in fact have not existed were it not widely held by Europeans that blacks belonged to an inferior race. Racism, thus, helped Europeans to pave way for the slave trade with which they exploited Africans to the worst. In fact, racial slavery resulted in the structural change in the world economy as it enriched Europeans at the cost of Africa such that they consequently established themselves as a superior race and imposed their cultures and religion on the African people. Yet today,

> European countries and others that involved in Africa try to forget the deaths and suffering caused by racial slavery, the blood spilled, mass murders and genocide, the severed hands and heads, the shattered families, and other crimes committed in Africa to extract wealth and capital (Jalata 2013: 2).

Europeans fail to understand the deeper meaning of the Shona proverb that *chinokanganwa idemo muti haukanganwi* (The offender and not the victim is the one who forgets so easily). I argue with Adam Hochschild (1998: 295), therefore, that 'forgetting one's participation in mass murder is not something passive; it is an active deed. In looking at the memories recorded by the early white conquistadors in Africa, we can sometimes catch the act of forgetting at the very moment it happens'. In fact, Europe should pay heed to the Zimbabwean

115

pan-Africanist, Vimbai Chivaura's plea that the people of Europe should not pretend to forget the wrongs they did to the African people. Instead, they have to pay reparation to the *ngozi* (the avenging spirit) of the African people.

Colonial terrorism

As noted by Giddens (1993: 528), 'the large majority of Third World societies are in areas that underwent colonial rule- in Asia, Africa and South America'. A series of critical questions can be raised: "Why formerly colonised countries are the poorest in the world when most of them stayed for centuries under the colonial rulers who purported to have been in a civilising enterprise? Is it because the former colonial settlers/European imperialists stole away the treasures of their former colonies to fuel Western economic development? Or is it because of poor governance in all the formerly colonised countries?"

Making an analysis of the economic consequences of colonialism by European powers on their colonies, Giddens (1993: 529-30) gave the following reasons:

i). Colonial possessions added to the political influence and power of the parent country and provided sites for military bases.

ii). Most Westerners also saw colonialism as a civilising enterprise, helping upgrade native peoples from their 'primitive' conditions. Missionaries wished to bring Christianity to the heathen, but by emphasising negativity on non-Western societies.

iii). There was an important economic motive. From the early years of Western expansion, food, raw materials and other goods were taken from the colonised areas to fuel Western economic development. Even where colonies were not acquired primarily for economic gain, the colonising country nevertheless almost always strove to achieve sufficient

116

economic return to cover the costs of its administration of the area.

I underscore Giddens' argument that Europe's colonising effect on Africa was dismal and helped to impoverish African states by draining their resources to enrich Europe, and continually 'crush African resistance by a ruthlessly systematic exploitation of the technological gap between European and African weaponry and military organisation' (Ganiage 1985: 157). The impoverishing of the African countries was aggravated by the general hatred of Africans by the European imperialists. Giddens (1993: 264) captures this aptly when he observes, 'the racist attitudes of European colonial settlers were almost everywhere more extreme in relation to blacks than other non-whites'. This is because Africans were considered markedly inferior to the Indians given that early views of Indians were cultural rather than racial: Indians were only seen as savages and uncivilised and not as inferior as the Africans.

I add that in many parts of the world, European imperialism had serious consequences on its colonies especially in Africa where the history of imperialism is so protracted that it cut through centuries. On this point, I remind and perhaps inform others that European imperialism in Africa did not start in the 15th century as many with limited knowledge of African history might think. Persians were perhaps the first Western imperialists on the African soils as these invaded parts of the continent some more than two thousand years before the 15th century Portuguese, English, Dutch/Boer and French imperialism. And, even before the 15th century, the Greeks with the help of Alexander the Great and later the Arabs, also terrorised some parts of Africa well before the Berlin Conference of 1884 which marked the beginning of the history of colonialism in Africa. Back to the consequences of European imperialism on the colonies, I should comment that because the European settlers introduced cash crops (such as tobacco, coffee, sugarcane etc.) to Africa to replace different systems (such as hunting and gathering, pastoralism etc.), the nutritional quality of the diets of the indigenous Africans was greatly compromised, and therefore levels of resistance to diseases were lowered. In fact, it is colonialism in Africa that gave way to cash crop economy as opposed to African traditional food farming, hunting and gathering thereby resulting in local food insecurity across the continent. It is only after cash crop production took over the local ways of production in Africa that malnutrition and diseases such as kwashiokor became a serious talk in many parts of the continent.

Illustrating how cultural subjugation of the [indigenous] peoples such as those in Africa by European imperialists resulted in severe malnutrition and massive deaths, Karl Polanyi (1944: 159-60, emphasis original) notes:

> The catastrophe of the native community, for example in Africa, is a direct result of the rapid and violent disruption of the basic institutions of the victim ... These institutions are disrupted by the very fact that a market economy is foisted upon an entirely differently organised community; labour and land are made into a commodity, which, again, is only a short formula for the liquidation of every ... cultural institution in an organic society.

This is seconded by Mike Davis who notes that in the process of eradicating famine from Europe, European imperialists accelerated famine and malnutrition-induced deaths in many other parts of the world such as Africa. Davis (2001: 9), thus, notes:

> Millions died, not outside the 'modern world system,' but in the very process of being forcibly incorporated into its economic and political structures. They died in the

golden age of Liberal Capitalism; indeed, many were murdered [...] by the theological application of the sacred principles of [Adam] Smith.

Besides, it should be underlined that Europeans during colonialism did not pre-occupy themselves with empowering and developing the indigenous [African] people economically. What they just wanted from the locals was their cheap labour and resources that allowed them to continue harvesting blood money and maximise their profits in very short periods of time. This explains why during and even after the colonial period most of the indigenous people in former European colonies, for example, remained poor and continued to use traditional methods of production in their agricultural adventures despite the runaway increases in populations. Most of these Africans either remained poor such that they could not afford machinery or without expertise to practice mechanised farming. In view of this observation, I argue that opportunities from the process of globalisation are and have always been limited to those with access to skills and training in the use of modern technologies to enhance development. In this regard, rural areas especially in non-industrialised societies as those in Africa are further prejudiced as such opportunities are rare if ever exist.

Also, the expansion of the Western imperial powers in the colonial era helped the spreading of certain deadly disease to other parts of the world such as Africa. As noted by Rene Dubos (1959), the expansion of the West in the colonial era took certain diseases into parts of the world where they had not previously existed. Dubos gives examples of smallpox, measles and typhus which were unknown to the indigenous populations of Central and South America before the Spanish conquest, French and English colonialists brought the aforementioned diseases to North America. Prior to this, the hunting and gathering communities of the Americas were not as subject to infectious diseases as Europe. This was the same with the African communities whose levels of risk from diseases such as malaria and sleeping sickness were lower than they subsequently became after the contact with Europeans: Africans, for example, in East Africa had large herds of cattle whereas Europeans failed to increase or even to maintain the same number of cattle as a result of the uncontrolled spread of tsetse fly. While mosquitoes and tsetse flies were indeed always a threat to the African communities, the communities had their own indigenous ways of dealing with the mosquitoes and tsetse flies which were despised by the colonial settlers. Besides, colonialism led to major changes to the African populations and how they related with their environments. Europeans, for example, introduced new farming methods which upset the whole ecosystem. It is through the imposition of new methods to replace the old one in all spheres of the African peoples' lives that colonialism declared and registered the demise of the African peoples' cultural, religious, and politico-economic autonomy.

Neo-imperialism

The theory of imperialism which was first advanced by the English historian, John Hobson, in his analysis of the Western states still has relevance today. In his theory, Hobson observed that majority of the population in the West were only able to afford to buy a relatively small proportion of goods that could be produced such that there was a constant striving both for new markets in which to sell and for ways of cheapening production by finding new sources of inexpensive raw materials and labour power in other parts of the world. This is what drives humanity towards imperialism, Hobson would say. By imperialism, Hobson (1965) meant the drive to conquer and subjugate other peoples, of which colonialism was one expression or result from these pressures towards external expansion.

In post-colonial era in Africa it is as late as 1998 that the Indigenous Knowledge for Development Programme was launched to help people learn from community based knowledge systems and development practices as well as to incorporate them into World Bank-supported programmes (World Bank 2004: vii). This connotes that as late as 1998, and even today, Indigenous Knowledge Systems are still largely ignored or at least have not yet been seriously considered and valued: Africa is still a victim of some Western and American imperial countries. There is ample evidence, through cases, that shows that Africa is still a victim of circumstances in as far as her indigenous knowledge systems are concerned. As, for instance, noted by Tom Suchanandan, an environmental legal expert in the National Indigenous Knowledge System Office under the Department of Science and Technology:

The African Union did an economic study in 2005 and it revealed at that time that Africa was losing between US$5, 6 billion and US$8 billion from the theft of its biodiversity ... Although it's difficult to quantify the losses, we can give indicators since 98% of patents held worldwide are held by developed countries while only 2 % are held by India and other developing countries (Sifelani Tsiko 2012: 2).

A critical analysis of the above quotation testifies to the fact that Africa is perhaps losing even more than US$8 billion as envisaged by Suchanandan. And, given the poor economic atmosphere prevailing in most of the African countries, I add that no African country, so far, is free from the losses to the Western world. Zimbabwe, for example, suffered losses to Switzerland in 1995. In as recent as 2010, South Africa recorded a number of accusations of bio-piracy, as has been captured by Regis Mafuratidze (cited in Tsiko 2012: 2):

The first 2010 South African bio-piracy case involved the illegitimate use of traditional knowledge surrounding the medicinal properties of pelargonium sidoides by Germany's Schwabe, and the second, the bio-prospecting on Honeybush and Rooibos by Swiss food giant Nestle without appropriate permits from the South African government.

I insist that the above testifies the fact that though the Convention on Biological Diversity (CBD) of 1993 and the Nagoya Protocol were established as instruments to control and guarantee the fair use and benefit of biodiversity or genetic resources to the communities they are found, the instruments appear to be ineffective. In fact, it remains clear that there is no strict system or framework to monitor bio-piracy and to regulate activities of multinationals most of which are from the North: most of the instruments or laws available are more of toothless dogs. In view of this reluctance at international level, it is beyond doubt that multinational companies will continue to make huge profits from Africa's biological wealth, and resist the idea of sharing the resources with the local communities who own them. No wonder scholars such as John Lonsdale (1985: 722) laments of Africa's loses to European imperialists: 'Everywhere the conquests of Africa brought similar paradoxes of public disaster and private profit in their train'. Such a disturbing situation calls for an urgent crafting and tabling of a development framework for Africa by Africans themselves to ensure that the continent doesn't continue losing millions of dollars to many of the Western countries and America. Genuine strict bio-piracy laws that protect poor [indigenous] communities should be put in place to police those countries or companies with exploitative tendencies.

I argue that the cases cited above are examples of acts of terrorism and imperialism by the West [through large business corporations] that for a long time have benefitted the economic development of Western countries while impoverishing much of the world. In fact with the end of the

Second World War and the unwavering for world peace by Civil Rights groups the world over, the Western imperial countries noted that warfare of guns and missiles was no longer tolerated by many in the world. As such, all the gimmicks that the Western countries are using to siphon and drain off resources from Africa are a clear testimony that modern warfare is no longer strictly and solely confined to the use of missiles and guns. In fact some ideas/theories, sophisticated technologies and gadgets from the Western world have been seen in the modern world impacting negatively on the survival of humankind, socio-economic development and peace in many parts of the world such as Africa. This is so because the Western countries have always drained off and siphoned resources from many parts of the world to enrich their respective countries. Large business corporations, thus, lead the way in exploiting the non-industrialised regions while enriching the so-called developed nations. In the post-colonial era in Africa, the Western countries have perpetuated their privileged position by ensuring total control of the terms and principles through world trade is carried on, and by ensuring control of influential international organisations such as the World Bank and International Monetary Fund. European imperial countries and America, thus, continue playing gimmicks on Africans to guarantee maintenance of their racialized capitalist world system and dominance over African societies.

Brain drain

Brain drain is one other problem that has haunted Africa for a long time now. Most of the people who leave the continent do so in search of 'greener pastures'. Most of the countries in the West pay more than what African countries do even for those people doing the same job and with the same qualifications. Many African governments cite problems of lack of resources and government funds as excuses for poor remunerations. Nevertheless, many African professionals who see themselves as being short-changed by their own governments do nothing except to leave for the greener pastures, especially in the Western world.

Yet while African governments are partly blamed for failing to curb brain drain on the continent, a critical analysis of world politics shows that as long as the systems that were created by Europe during slavery and colonialism are maintained, Africa will continue suffering the same problem and many others for a long time to come. These systems include the control of international economic organisations such as World Bank, International Monetary Fund as well as the continued siphoning of Africa's resources and use of lethal violence, among others. In this light, I argue that brain drain is an economic weapon of the developed world, especially the Western countries, which will ensure the continued deprivation and impoverishment of the African continent.

The above point is further proven by the gesture that many Western countries and the United States of America (USA) have taken over the years in relation to skilled workers and exceptionally intellectually gifted students from Africa. In countries such as Canada, Australia and the USA, only to mention but a few, the respective governments through their departments of Foreign Affairs facilitate the issuing out of permanent resident permits and what they call 'Green Cards' to skilled workers. Likewise, those students from the African continent who excel exceptionally well in their academic endeavours, especially at Advanced Level are normally lured to come and study in the Western universities after which they are often offered permanent residents and very good jobs. This is to ensure that they forget about Africa their motherland. Thus instead of coming back to Africa to help develop their motherland, they are enticed to stay and enrich the West. These are some of the strategies that the West and America are using to ensure that Africa remains poor and an underdeveloped continent.

Financial imperialism

In the past, particularly during slavery and colonialism in Africa, European imperialists conquered the African people through the use of 'advanced military hardware'. Now that war is being discouraged everywhere in the world through the works of humanitarian or civil organisations, the European imperial countries have also changed their strategies to pry over Africa. Financial imperialism through debts and controlled [financial] aid – aid used as a means to a manipulative end – has become the 'new' weapon used by Europe to reconquer Africa. By financial imperialism, I mean a system through which 'giant' or developed economies exercise authoritarian control over 'weaker' or developing economies in order to exploit them (the developing economies). In this equation, the giant economies are the American and European imperial countries while the developing economies are the African countries. This exploitative relationship results in a gulf between the developed economies and the developing economies. One may wonder how this exactly happens. The answer is very simple: through the creation of the 'developing economies monster' – debt and controlled financial aid. The question that troubles many of us is: "Why modern societies continue to create monsters – systems that perpetuate the enrichment of developed economies and impoverishment of the developing economies? I argue that such system as the *debt tactic* is a continuation and overlap of the colonial system and modern society controlled by the Western imperial countries. Debt, for example, ensures that developing economies divert all their profits from local development projects to interest payments into the financial banks of the developed economies. In fact, attention of the developing economies, instead of being invested towards local development projects, is directed towards debt paying. 'Real' development to the developing economies, therefore, remains a tantalising process that is never fulfilled or realised. This keeps Africa frozen in the so-called Third World bracket or even worse such that investment towards healthcare, education and industry becomes difficult or an obvious impossibility. To this effect, I would like to believe that if the African debt (that was greatly created due to the colonial legacy on the continent) is cancelled and with good governance on the continent, the World Bank, International Monetary Fund, United Nations, European Union and other such organisations would not need to provide any more financial aid to Africa. This is because Africa as a continent is flourishing with resources (oil, coal, gas, diamond, gold, water, land, etc.) which if properly managed could change her face in no time in terms of industrialising the continent and investment in healthcare and education.

In search of a development framework for Africa

The merit of African epistemologists and custodians of the so-called indigenous knowledge is that they are very much willing to share their knowledge, and even to integrate it with other knowledge forms for better results. The research carried out by the World Bank, for instance, revealed that:

> Communities [African indigenous people] are quite willing, indeed eager, to combine global knowledge and modern technology with their indigenous knowledge and institutions to obtain better results. Traditional Birth Attendants in the Iganga District of Uganda, for example, use modern walkie-talkies to refer critical cases to the public health system, thus contributing to reducing maternal mortality substantially, one of the MDGs (World Bank 2004: vii).

Taking it from the aforementioned observation, I propose the following as the African framework of development that could help to easy the tapestry of African development problems:

i). From the quotation above by the World Bank, it is clear that [African] communities already have their own starting point to stir up and fuel development: in fact communities can empower themselves to manage their own development in their respective localities and the larger context of globalisation if their [indigenous] knowledge is seriously considered. Reinforcing the same line of thinking, the World Bank (1998: 16) has described the role that indigenous knowledge plays in both local and global development:

> Knowledge is critical for development, because everything we do depends on knowledge. Simply to live, we must transform the resources we have into the things we need, and that takes knowledge. And if we want to live better tomorrow than today, if we want to raise living standards as a household or as a country-and improve our health, better educate our children, and preserve our common environment – we must do more than simply transform more resources, for resources are scarce. We must use those resources in ways that generate ever-higher returns to our efforts and investments. That, too, takes knowledge and ever-greater proportion to our resources.

Building on practices or knowledge that communities already have always has a tremendous [positive] effect in scaling up development process and ensuring sustainable development of the community in question. In non-Western societies, it is only unfortunate that in the past such practices have either been misunderstood or demonised and despised by European researchers, explorers and missionaries. In relation to misunderstanding of African [indigenous] practices (embedded in their IKSs), Gyekye succinctly explains part of the reason why they were misunderstood. He thus notes that in Africa:

> Science has been mixed with religion, so that what could have become scientific knowledge open to everyone, became a sort of a secret knowledge, open only to priests, spiritual healers, and others who are traditionally acknowledged as the custodians of the secrets and truths of nature (Gyekye 1996: 139).

Thinking in a Western framework that science and religion are two distinct realms, some European scholars were made to think that Africans had no science but superstition. This misunderstanding and misrepresenting of African practices have been worsened by the fact that the first crop of researchers from the West such as explorers, travellers, and missionaries were either in a mission to demonise Africa and the African people or had tight schedules which could not allow them to spend periods long enough to merit clear understanding and, therefore, authentic results about the [African] people being studied. What the Kenyan scholar, Jess Mugambi, observes in relation to the responsibility of African scholars can be applied in this context. Mugambi (2005: 28, emphasis original) observes that:

> It is the responsibility of African scholars to write and publish textbooks for the courses they teach. We have a rather sad situation in Africa, in which we teach in the African cultural context, and use books intended for use in other cultures especially from the Western world. Only African scholars can deal with this ironical situation. It is not enough to complain about cultural alienation and academic irrelevance. We have to become part of the solution, rather than part of the problem.

The underlying point thus remains, that practices that [African] communities already hold should be seriously considered and taken aboard in the global development process: the global notion of development ought to be balanced with the Western, African, Northern and Eastern notions of development equally considered.

ii). It should be noted that by continuing with neo-imperialism through the perpetuation of the demonization of some [African] indigenous knowledge systems and beliefs, draining off and siphoning resources from Africa, the West has (and continues to) created a dependency syndrome for African countries. As the dependency theory itself suggests, the uneven development across the world that has been propelled by European countries and America have made the industrialised countries to play a dominant role with the Third World countries being dependent on them. This dependency involves the reliance of Third World countries on Western relief funds, on selling raw materials/cash crops, and on providing human resources to the developed world. This inhibit developing countries from graduating into developed ones; hence my argument that Africa should move away from a situation whereby Europe and the United States of America continue sacrificing her quietly like a sheep being led to the alter. Action should be taken to actively counterbalance the Western and American economic dominance and hegemony through rigorous campaigns for her indigenous knowledge systems and the establishment of a firm industrial base. This will allow the creation of a new dispensation whereby Africa will graduate from being a *dependent* to a *self-dependent* continent. Once this happens, there is high likelihood of a shift of economic powers from the West to Africa especially given that *resource-wise* Africa is one of the richest continents in the world.

iii) Currently, there is anomie in Africa. Taking it from Emile Durkheim's (1858-1917), by anomie, I mean the undermining of traditional norms and standards (or values) in a given area of social life of a society or group without replacing them with new ones. I say this because besides the World Bank and International Monetary Fund's economic programmes imposed now and then on African economies, there seems to be no clear standards (or what I refer to as the African framework of development) set by Africans themselves and for Africa to guide and determine development pace and trend. This is resulting in 'disorientation' and indeed limits people's development capacities. I give one example of industrialised societies where the generally held value is 'making money'. The means [or framework] for attaining this value include self-discipline and hard work. This should not be interpreted to mean that Africans lack discipline or are lazy. The argument here is that for development on the continent to progress, there is need by African governments to identify or set general values which act as framework for development. Currently, there seems to be undermining of the values of egalitarianism and/or communalism in Africa unfortunately even by some Africans, yet there is no effort to replace those values (which served Africa for centuries now) with new ones. This takes people off track as some are left confused on which values to embrace instead thereby undermining community survival, general economic development and public safety. Yet the truth is there are many aspects of development that African traditional culture has that should be promoted and even 'sold' to other non-African societies. A good example is that of an African [traditional] business person. It is traditionally known in many African traditional cultures that an African business person can sell his [her] goods and services at any time of the day so long as there is a customer. This is the opposite in Western cultures where everything seems to be timed. While this aspect of the African culture is positive business-wise in so far as it helps to boost up one's profits, the aspect seems to be unrecognised worse still promoted within and beyond the boundaries of African societies. I argue here that this one aspect of the African culture that could be promoted within and in other cultures to strengthen the African culture and to boost global economic development.

Another important business aspect in the African [traditional] culture is that of extended family. Extended family being one aspect of the African communalist culture is often criticised by Western countries that are capitalistic in nature. They seem to believe that extended family is a burden that compromises one's capacity to make profits yet there is a positive element of this aspect that they don't see the same way one from an African [traditional] culture would. Extended family sometimes provides free labour to the business person. This in no doubt enhances the business person's capacity to make more profit. Besides, extended family provides the business person with comfort and morale to excel in business. Unfortunately, these important aspects are rarely recognised worse still promoted in other cultures to strengthen the African culture. I believe that if many of the already existing aspects of African traditional culture are strengthened and promoted in other societies, Africa would be able to stand as an equal contributor of the global culture or the so-called globalisation. Unfortunately, some African leaders are failing to read between the lines to the extent that they embrace foreign values more than they do their own [African] values. What they don't see is the fact that in the process they forfeit their sovereignty and even integrity as a people. Yet if at least some of the values of the African people are promoted [willy-nilly] in other cultures, this would enable Africa to be in charge of her own destiny, and indeed go a long way in simultaneously fostering her own socio-economic development while promoting that of the global world.

iv). The other important thing that African governments should do as a matter of urgency is to establish rigorous and organised cultural and development institutions that address problems facing global societies particularly Third World

Countries. These institutions should be fully supported, in terms of funding and equipment, by African institutes to ensure that they carry out research in the interest of Africa. Otherwise if externally funded, the institutions' research objectives and vision could be high jacked and derailed from the track. I acknowledge that some strides towards this position have already been taken but the rate at which this is being done is disheartening. In fact, very few African countries already have cultural and development institutions that address the aforementioned problems. Yet such a move would help tremendously in providing cultural diets that are nutritious (instead of genetically modified foods) and accessible, in providing traditional medicines that are not only locally available but cost effective, and in providing indigenous traditional games for entertaining both the young and the old. This will help greatly to stem out cultural atrophy in Africa and socio-economically empower Africans such that they become self-reliant and independent.

v). Lastly, industrialisation seems Africa's ultimate solution to bridge the gap between poverty and industrialisation. Currently, the problem with Africa is that while she is endowed with natural resources (and raw materials) of all kinds, she lacks the refinement capacity to process those resources/raw materials into finished products. Most of Africa's mineral refinement (such as that of diamond, gold etc.), for example, is done in the West or the East. This means that Africa is losing a lot of money in this whole process given that finished products are always more expensive than the raw materials. Once Africa develops the capacity to build her own industries, she will graduate into a first world power, and ceases to depend on America and Europe.

I should underscore, however, that the suggestions elaborated in this book are not the only strategies that could help boost up development and to stem out the tide of cultural atrophy in Africa. Many other strategies can possibly be explored to deal with the global challenges highlighted throughout the pages of this book.

Also, I must underline that this book is not prescribing a complete retreat into pre-colonial African practices and traditions as this will be anachronistic or rather advocating for stasis. Also, there is historical evidence to show that an attempt to return to the pre-colonial African heritage that manifested itself in the philosophy of *Negritude*[2] did not appeal to the masses in the 1960s, when even the atmosphere was highly charged against colonial domination (see Dikirr, 2005). During the 1960s, *Negritude* did not appeal much to the masses due perhaps to the fact that its proponents could not explain in clear and convincing terms to the people what it was meant for, or perhaps because the people of the time thought it was not the right response to their needs. In contemporary Africa, the combination of Western and Christian influence, together with the effects of globalisation (particularly global capitalism) make such a transition even more untenable. On this note, I register my consciousness of Dikirr's (2005, p. 45) argument that 'in today's Africa, a discourse that is wholly predicated on the people's past heritage, especially their alleged spiritual and closeness to the land, will be of little value'. Although I agree with Dikirr to some extent, I insist that for Africa to develop independently, there is urgent need to bring to the fore what the indigenous methods and practices of African people involve, and to examine the extent to which these indigenous

---

[2] The major motivating force for the Negritude Movement was, according to Mafeje, a protest against 'the disillusionment and resentment of the dehumanizing oppression of colonial domination and suppression of the black people' (see Mafeje 1992). Negritude was championed by Africa leaders and scholars such as Leopold Senghor, Cheikh Anta Diop, Kwame Nkrumah among others. 'According to Ali Mazrui [2003], the concept of negritude, the celebration of African identity and uniqueness, was invented in Paris by the Martinique poet and philosopher, Aime Cesaire. However, its most famous proponent in Africa according to Mazrui was the founder-president of independent Senegal, Leopold Senghor' (cited in Dirkirr, 2005, p.118).

methods and practices could initiate, stir, complement or blend with Western scientific means of stirring development for the benefit of the people of Africa.

Chapter 6

Africa's new relationship with China: A breakthrough for Africa?

Introduction

The socio-economic, cultural, political and military relations between Africa and China though date back to as far as 202 BC and AD 220 (Snow 1988) took a new dimension after the demise of European colonial administration in Africa especially since the late 1990s. As revealed by Le Monde Diplomatique (2005), trade between China and Africa increased by 700 % during the 1990s. It is estimated to have increased even more sharply since the year 2000 when the Forum on China-Africa Cooperation (FOCAC) was established (in October 2000) as an official forum to strengthen the relationship between Africa and China especially in trade. This official forum saw China becoming Africa's largest trading partner, a reality that has resulted in the grumbling of many European countries (as well as the United States of America) that previously benefitted from trade with Africa. The United Kingdom and the United States of America (USA), for instance, have since raised serious concern over the People's Republic of China's economic, political and military role in Africa. The concern was especially aggravated by the Ministry of Foreign Affairs of the People's Republic of China's (2002) categorical emphasis on China's developmental aid to Africa and his statement that China and Africa are swiftly moving towards 'joint efforts to maintain the lawful rights of developing countries and push forward the creation of a new, fair and just political and economic order in the world.' Yet while China's critics (e.g. David Blair, 2007), the USA and European countries continue to register their suspicion on the renewed relationship between Africa and China, the latter has always defended her stance on Africa. During the 2008 socio-economic and political crisis in Zimbabwe, for example, a Chinese Senior Official defended his country's aid to African countries such as Zimbabwe and Sudan thereby resisting Europe and America's imposed sanctions on Zimbabwe in response to the latter's alleged violations of human rights. Endorsing China's humanitarian stance on Africa, Liu Guijin, China's special envoy for African affairs had this to say of China (Financial Times 2014):

> While we are not satisfied with the environment in many developing countries, we don't attach political conditions [to aid]. We have to realise the political and economic environments are not ideal. But we don't have to wait for everything to be satisfactory or human rights to be perfect.

On the same thrust, the Assistant Director- General of the Department of Aid to Foreign Countries at the Chinese Ministry of Commerce, Song Wei (2013) in her recent lecture on China's Perspective on the Development of sub-Saharan countries, noted that unlike the West that continually calls for 'reform in return for investment/aid', China perceived its relationship with African countries as a partnership offering mutual benefits.

In view of this scenario, I offer in this chapter, my view on the China – African relationship and how the relationship should be monitored to ensure mutual benefit between the two actors. In this regard, I propose guidelines to be followed to avoid the historical asymmetrical relationship that existed between Africa and Europe until the demise of colonial administration in Africa.

Historical background to Africa-China Relationship

The socio-economic, political, military and cultural relationship between China and Africa is not something new. While little is known concerning the relationship between China and Africa prior to the advent of European colonialism in Africa, there is ample evidence that the continent of Africa always related with China especially on trade. According to Philip Snow (1988), Africa and China's trade connections, sometimes through third parties, date back to far as 202 BC and AD 220. Some archaeological excavations at Mogadishu (Somalia) and Kilwa (Tanzania) have recovered several coins from China, majority of the coins of which date to the Song Dynasty which is one of the most ancient dynasties in China (Pankhurst 1961: 268). Freeman-Grenville (1975) also reveals that in as early as 1226, Chao Jukua, commissioner of foreign trade of the Fujian Province of China, completed his Chu-fan-chih (Description of Barbarous Peoples) which he discusses Ts'ong-pa (Zanzibar) and Pi-P'a-lo (Somalia).

Many other scholars also highlight the medieval contacts, particularly in the 14th century, between China and Africa when Ibn Battuta, the Moroccan scholar and traveller arrived in China (see Keat, 2004), Sa'id of Mogadishu, the Somali scholar and explorer reached China and when the Ming Dynasty voyages of the Chinese, Zheng He, arrived the coast of Mozambique (see CCTV, 2002). Some other accounts (for instance by Eliot, 1966) mention Chinese ships sinking near Lamu Island in Kenya in 1415 resulting in the surviving Chinese settling in the island and married local women. To buttress this information, archaeological excavations on the island and in some Kenyan villages have recovered porcelains made during the Tang Dynasty (618-907). As China Daily (07/11/2005) and York (2005) revealed, local tradition on Kenyan coast maintains that 20 shipwrecked Chinese sailors, possibly part of the famous Zheng's fleet, washed up on shore some hundreds of years ago were permitted to settle by local groups after having killed a dangerous python. These Chinese people were converted to Islam and later on married local women. Some DNA tests conducted on one of the women in the Kenyan coast confirmed that she was of the Chinese descent.

The evidence of ancient China-Africa relations is not only found in eastern Africa, but southern Africa. Melanie Yap and Daniel Leong Man, in their famous book: *Colour, confusions and concessions: The history of Chinese in South Africa*, also cite Chu Ssu-pen, a Chinese mapmaker in 1320 who is believed to have had the first southern African map drawn on one of his maps. Also, some ceramics (porcelain dated 960-1279 AD) found at archaeological excavations in South Africa and Zimbabwe dated back to Song Dynasty of China (see Perry, 2008). Besides all this evidence, it is well known that until a few years ago, there lived north of Cape Town, groups of people with light coloured skin (Mongolian features) who spoke a language tonally similar to the Chinese Mandarin who called themselves Awatwa (abandoned people). These people traced their origins to the 13th century Chinese sailors who were part of Zheng He's team that explored Africa's east coast between 1405 and 1433 (see Perry, 2008).

In the contemporary times, China-Africa relations dates back to the late 1950s when China signed the first official bilateral trade agreement with Algeria, Egypt, Somalia, Guinea, Sudan and Morocco. During this time, China cultivated economic, political and military ties with many African countries. Most importantly, China provided technical and military support to many African countries and liberation movements in an effort to encourage wars of national liberation and revolution which saw majority of the African countries liberated from the European colonial rule in the 1960s through the 1970s and 1980s (see also Muekalia 2004). Among the most notable early projects in Africa financed and built by China was the 1, 860 km Tazara Railway (known among the local people as the Freedom Railway) linking Zambia and Tanzania constructed between 1970 and 1975 (Brautigam 2010). In Sudan, the Chinese government helped construct the 20 m wide and 440 m long China-Sudan Friendship Bridge across the Nile River (the largest river in Africa), which is the first bridge in Sudan that connects the western to the eastern part of the country. In the deal, China charged a token US$ 20 million for the bridge with the total cost to Sudan (the host country) for the China-Sudan Friendship Bridge (opened 17 January 2008) being US$ 10 million. A similar bridge to cross the Mississippi River in the United States costs a US$ 1, 6 billion (Martian2 2013).

Health-wise, Africa has also benefitted significantly since the 1960s. As Drew Thomson reveals, between 1960 and 2005, more than 15, 000 Chinese medical doctors – a medical team known as Yiliaodui – have been sent to Africa to help treat different cases in more than 47 countries treating more than 170 million patients during this period (see also China Daily News 2 Nov 2006; www.china.org.cn).

China's business activities in Africa: A breakthrough for the African continent?

While some people view the involvement of China in African business activities as a positive move in boosting Africa's economy, some countries (especially in the West and America), scholars and business people in Africa, think otherwise. The latter, for example, consider the involvement of China in Africa as a move that thwarts the hopes and aspirations of the African business people by taking away opportunities that were in fact theirs.

Commenting on the positives, reveals that as a gesture to show her genuine friendship with Africa, China is offering unconditional and low-rate credit lines (rates at 1.5 % over 15

139

years to 20 years) (Le Monde Diplomatique 2005; Financial Times 2014), a move that has overtaken Western partners whose loans are more restricted and conditional.

Besides, since 2000, more than US$ 10 billion in debt owed by African nations to the People's Republic of China has been cancelled (Le Monde Diplomatique 2005), making China a better partner as compared to Africa's longstanding partners like Europe and the United States of America. Yet such gestures have never been enough to silence critics from within the African continent and the West who feel China's business activities in Africa are exploitative.

Commenting on a recent business partnership between China and Angola, an independent economist, Jose Cerqueira pointed out: 'There is a condition in the loan [offered to Angola by China] that 30 % will be subcontracted to Angolan firms, but that still leaves 70 % which will not. Angolan businessmen are very worried about this, because they don't get the business, and the construction sector is one in which Angolans hope they can find work' (see Le Monde Diplomatique, 2005). In Mozambique, there has also been criticism of too many Chinese workers taking jobs that should go to Mozambicans as the Chinese firms normally favour Chinese employees (see Shinn 2012).

Recent studies have also revealed that most of China's raw materials such as mineral ores, petroleum, and agricultural products, come from Africa. For example, one-third of China's oil supplies comes from the African continent, mainly from Angola and Nigeria (Alessi and Hanson 2012; Linebaugh and Oster 2006). Besides, Benin and the Sahel countries of Burkina Faso and Mali supply up to 20 % of China's cotton needs. On the other hand, Cote d'Ivoire supplies most of China's cocoa needs while Kenya, Namibia and Mozambique supply coffee, fish and timber respectively to China (Financial Times 2014). It is worth noting that most of these exports to China are made in exchange to packages of aid and loan as well as infrastructure building. Yet, while it is acknowledged that China is doing significant investment and development of Africa's burgeoning oil sector, China is facing growing international criticism over its allegedly exploitative business practices coupled with a failure to promote and cultivate good governance and human rights in Africa.

Some reports indicate that Chinese funding usually guarantees a Chinese company will get the tender for the project (Shinn 2012). There is evidence to support this claim based on the past experiences in many countries in Africa. The 1, 860 km Tazara Railway (also known as the Tanzam or the Freedom Railway) connecting the port of Dar es Salam in Tanzania with the town of Kapiri Mposhi in Zambia's Central Province was, for instance, constructed by the Chinese company, China Civil Engineering Construction Corporation (Brautigam 2010: 163). The Tanzanian national stadium that hosted the Beijing Olympic torch relay in April 2008, though jointly financed by China and Tanzania, was constructed by a Chinese Engineering Company (CCTV 2009). The Sudanese-Chinese Friendship Bridge, which is the biggest bridge of its own kind, was also constructed by a Chinese construction contractor called China's Jilin International Economic and Technical Corporation (Tong 2009). In Mozambique, Maputo national stadium (known as Estadio do Zimpeto, inaugurated in 2011) built with funds from the Chinese government was constructed by the Chinese company, Anhui Foreign Economic Construction Group (personal communication 2011). The implication that China gives tender of the projects she finances to companies from China is that China takes back by her left hand what she gives by her right hand.

Another worrying observation is that most of China's exports to Africa are largely manufactured goods. Besides that China continues to enjoy Africa's raw materials such as agricultural products and petroleum. In Sudan, for example, by 1996 the state-owned China National Petroleum Corporation

(CNPC) was pumping oil from Block 6, which straddles Sudan's Kordofan and South Darfur states and whose production it controls almost exclusively as it owns 95 % stake (Foundation for Defence of Democracies 2014). In view of exports to Africa, in 2011 alone, for instance, China exported manufactured goods to Africa worth US$93 billion with Chinese-made products such as machinery, electrical, armament/fire arms, footwear/clothing, and consumer goods increased by 17, 5% to reach US$ 30, 9 billion during the first five months of the year 2012 (King 2012). Such a relationship where one exports only finished goods while importing only raw materials from the same trading partner is exploitative. It is exploitative because finished products are always more expensive than unfinished goods or raw materials. Instead, China should invest significantly in setting up processing facilities in African countries and in training African citizens to boost the continent's manufacturing industry such that the former could also make imports proportional to those of Africa. This would allow a symmetrical relationship between China and Africa, a relationship that would reverse what scholars like Deborah Brautigam's (2010) description of China's help to Africa as "the dragon's gift".

I should also point out that while China is helping Africa in building infrastructure, the disappointing thing is that most of the workers involved in the construction of the infrastructures come directly from China. During the construction of the Tazara Railway that links Zambia and Tanzania, for example, some 500. 000 Chinese engineers and workers were brought to the continent to complete the project (Brautigam 2010). In Mozambique, there was a public uproar as most of the Chinese companies (especially in the construction and restaurant sectors) in the country abuse Mozambican workers while others employ mostly people of Chinese descent thereby taking away jobs meant for Mozambicans (see also Southern Africa Resource Watch 2012; Bosten 2006). What this means is that the locals who should benefit from such projects through employment are sometimes even impoverished as such constructions sometimes destroy people's gardens, fields and plantations which are in fact sources of their livelihoods. Thus, while railway (as with dam construction) is a worthwhile project, sometimes the locals fail to realise the benefit it brings if the investors do not benefit them through employment among other such gestures.

Besides, if one is to be critical of China's assistance to Africa it comes to light that what sometimes appears to be humanitarian aid comes with a price even heavier than what one could imagine. While it is a historical fact that the Chinese government helped construct the 20 m wide and 440 m long China-Sudan Friendship Bridge across the Nile River (the largest river in Africa), which is the first bridge in Sudan that connects the western to the eastern part of the country, this came with a heavy price. The US$ 20 million token charged by China to help constructing the bridge could have been a move to silence the Sudan government on the oil explorations that China has been enjoying for years now. As revealed by the Foundation for Defence of Democracies (2014), by 1996 the state-owned China National Petroleum Corporation (CNPC) was pumping oil from Block 6, which straddles Sudan's Kordofan and South Darfur states and whose production it controls almost exclusively as it owns 95 % stake. As further revealed by the Foundation for Defence of Democracies, CNPC acquired a 40 % stake in the Greater Nile Petroleum Operating Company, which holds concessions in Blocks 1, 2 and 4, and 41 % stake in the Petrdar Operating Company, which has holdings in Blocks 3 and 7. CNPC also holds a one-third share of the Red Sea Petroleum Operating Company which controls Block 15. Similar experiences have been observed recently in Mozambique where China is allegedly enjoying the exploration of the Indian waters (including that of the precious Sharks China is allegedly fishing illegally) and many others natural resources in return to construction of infrastructure such as roads and stadiums in the country. The construction of Tazara Railway linking Zambia and Tanzania between 1970 and 1975 was also done at a time China was actively seeking diplomatic support in the Third World against both the United States and the Soviet Union (Jung Chang and Jon Halliday, ny; see also Altorfer-Ong, 2009). All these are direct benefits being enjoyed by China which could help to explain why more often than not, the latter (China) opts to help Africa at what some people would think is a zero or minimal cost. I argue from these revelations that what China gives to Africa is much less than what she harvests and takes away from Africa.

Also, to show that China's interests in Africa has some strings attached, a number of Chinese citizens in some African countries have been caught stealing, bribing or illegally exploiting natural resources. In 2007, for example, Mozambique seized 531 containers of illegal log exports valued at US$ 7 million purchased by Chinese companies (Shinn 2012). In view of such experiences, I argue that African countries should be critical of their relationship with China. Otherwise, Africa will continue losing more resources to China through poaching and other illegal dealings.

Conclusion

Although international relations and diplomacy as concepts are deeply unpopular among majority of the citizens especially the rural folk, the aforementioned continue to permeate development in most state-run business and development interventions in many African countries. The case in point is the historical relationship between China and Africa. Throughout history, China has extended its relations to Africa in military, cultural, political and most importantly business activities. These relations, especially the economic ties between

Africa and China grew significantly in the past two decades, making China the biggest business partner of Africa since the year 2008. While the relations have allegedly benefitted both China and Africa in many different ways, critics have argued that the relations are asymmetrical in favour of China. China, thus, has faced mounting criticism from some scholars, the United States of America and the West who cite China's economic interest in Africa as exploitative and tantamounting to neo-colonialism. In this chapter, I have discussed Africa-China's longstanding relationship, a relationship that dates as far as 202 BC. The analysis made from different studies across the African continent has suggested that China benefits more from Africa than it ploughs back. Basing on this analysis, substantiated with data and case studies from different countries in the African continent, I have argued that the interests of China in Africa are highly suspicious: It is a relationship that should be handled with caution especially by the African governments, otherwise, it mirrors the European-African relationship during Europe's colonial adventures in Africa.

Bibliography

Aborishade, F. 2002. Effects of globalisation on social and labour practices in privatised enterprises in Nigeria, *A Research Report Submitted to The Centre for Advanced Social Sciences*, Port Harcourt, Nigeria.

Adler, N.J. 1991. *International dimensions of organisation behaviour,* Belmont, CA' Wadsworth.

Agha, R. 2003.*The Impact of a amass media campaign on personal risk perception, perceived self-efficacy and on other behavioural predictors,* AIDS Care.

Akande, W. 2002. *The drawback of cultural globalisation,* Yellowtimes.

Allafrica.com, Mozambique-China trade continues to grow, Maputo: Mozambique. (Retrieved 2 July 2014).

Alessi, C. and Hanson, S. (8/02/2012). *Expanding China-Africa oil ties,* Council on Foreign Relations.

Ali, A. 2009.Comentario de situação de educação, Available at:*www.mec.gov.mz,*/Ministerio da Educação e Cultura de Moçambique, (Accessed on 20/02/2010).

Altieri, M. A. 1995. *Agroecology: The science of sustainable agriculture,* 2nd Edition, London: IT Publications.

Altorfer-Ong, A. 2009. Tanzanian freedom and Chinese friendship in 1965: Laying the tracks for the Tanzam rail link, *London School of Law*, pp. 655-670.

Asante, K.W. 2000. *Zimbabwe Dance: Rhythmic Forces, Ancestral Voices-An Aesthetic Analysis,* Trenton: African World Press.

147

Awolalu, J. O. 1991. African traditional religion as an academic discipline, In: Uka, E. M. (Ed). *Readings in African traditional religion: Structure, meaning, relevance, future*, Peter Lang: New York.

Awuah-Nyamekye, S. 2009. Women's Participation in the Ritual of Worship in African Traditional Religion. *The Drumspeak: International Journal of Research in the Humanities' of Arts Faculty of University of Cape Coast*, Vol. 2, No.3 (December), pp.53-79.

Baldick, C. 2001. *The Concise Oxford Dictionary of Literary Terms*, 2nd Ed. Oxford: Oxford UP.

Barker, R. E. 1994.*Education and related concepts*, College Press Publishers, Harare.

Bastian,A.(Ed).(27/01/2009),EncyclopediaBritanica,*http://www .britanica.com/EBchecked/topics/55606/Adolf-Bastian* .

Benedict, E. T. 1959. *An anthropologist at work; Writings of Ruth Benedict*, Boston, MA: Houghton Mifflin.

Benedict, R. O. G. 1983. *Imagined Reflections on the origin and spread of nationalism*, Verso, London.

Biko, Steve. 1978. *I write what I like*, Heinemann, London.

Blair, D. 2007. *Why China is trying to colonise Africa*, Telegraph.co.uk, (Retrieved 02/07/2014).

Blake, P. 2009. 'What's In a Name? Your Link to the Past,' *BBC*, London.

Boas, F. 'The methods of anthropology', In George Stocking Jr. (Ed) (1940).*Race, Language and Culture*, Chicago University Press.

Bourdillon, M.F.C. 1976. *The Shona Peoples: An ethnography of the contemporary Shona, with special reference to their religion*, Mambo Press: Gweru, Zimbabwe.

Bosten, E. 2009. China's engagement in the construction industry of southern Africa: The case of Mozambique, Asian and other Drivers of Global Change, Institute of Development Studies.

Bower, A. (05/07/2007). 'Mozambique Culture: It is just different', Accessed on the 23 March 2010.

Brauutigam, D. 2010. *The dragon's gift: The real story of China in Africa*, Oxford University Press: Oxford.

Brodnicka, M. 2003. "When theory meets practice: undermining the principles of tradition and modernity in Africa", J. African Philosophy, Issue 2. Bureau of African Affairs, (Accessed 23/04/2010). Available at: http://www.africaknowledgeproject.org/index.php/jap/article/view/12.

Cabral, Amilcar. 1974. *Return to the source,* Monthly Review Press: New York.

CCTV, 2002. Zheng He's voyages, China Central Television: China.

CCTV. (16/02/2009). Tanzania largest beneficiary of Chinese aid in Africa, China Central Television: China.

Césaire, Aime. 2001. *Notebook of a return to the native land,* Wesleyan University Press: Middletown.

Chakaipa, P. 1961. *Rudo Ibofu,* Mambo Press, Gweru.

Characterisation, Http://en.wikipedia.org/wiki/character_arts, (Retrieved on 8 July 2010).

149

Chennels, A. 1995. "Rhodesian discourse, Rhodesian novels and the Zimbabwe liberation war", in Bhebe, N. and Ranger, T. (Eds), Society in Zimbabwe's Liberation War, pp.102–29. Harare: University of Zimbabwe Publications.

Chibatamoto, P. P. 1993. K.A.P. of traditional healers in relation to AIDS & *'runyoka'* in Zimbabwe, *International Conference on AIDS*, Blair Research Laboratory, Harare, Zimbabwe. Retrieved from: http://gateway.nih.gov/ (accessed on 16 May 2010).

Childs, P. and Fowler, R. 2006. *The Routledge Dictionary of Literary Terms,* London and New York: Routledge.

China Daily News. (11/07/2005). Mwamaka Sharifu: Descendant of Chinese sailor? Ministry Press Releases, China.

China Daily News. (2/11/2006). China medical teams continue to help Africa, Ministry Press Releases, China.

Christain Science Monitor, 2009. 'China boosts African economies, offering a second opportunity'.

Churchland, P. M. 1984. *Matter and Consciousness,* Cambridge, The MIT Press.

Daily Gazette Newspaper, Harare: Zimbabwe (8 March 1994).

Daily Gazette Newspaper, Harare: Zimbabwe (10 April 1994).

Daily Sun Newspaper, South Africa (4 October 2013).

Davies, S., McCallie, E., Simonsson, E., Lehr, J I., & Duensing, S. 2009. Discussing dialogue: perspectives on the value of science dialogue events that do not inform policy, *Public Understanding of Science*, 18(3): 338–353.

Davis, M. 2001. *Late Victorian holocausts: El Nino famines and the making of the Third World*, Verso: London.

Dikirr, P. M. 2005. Africa's Environmental Crisis: Unmapped Terrain, Existing Challenges and Possible Solutions, *PhD Thesis*, Binghamton University, State of New York.

DoktorSnake. 2010. Africa: Land of magic and sorcery, Retrieved from: http://en.wikipedia.org/wiki/Africa (accessed on 2 May 2010).

Dubos, R. 1959. *Mirage of health*, Doubleday Anchor: New York.

Eade, D. (Ed) 2002. *Culture and development*, Oxford: Oxfam GB.

Ekwuru, G. 1999. *The pangs of an African culture in travail*, Totan publishers limited: Owerri.

Elaine, A. & Savona, G. 1991. *Theatre as Sign-System: A semiotics of text and performance*, London and New York: Routledge.

Eliot, C. 1966. *The East African Protectorate*, Routledge, London.

ENotes on Shakespeare, (Accessed 23 March 2014), Available at: *http://www.enotes.com/shakespeare-quotes*.

Falola, T. 2003. *The power of African cultures*, University of Rochester Press, New York: USA.

Falola, T. 2002. *Key Events in African History: A Reference Guide*, Greenwood Press: Westport.

Financial Times, 2014. *Africa-China trade*, United Kingdom.

Foundation for Defence of Democracies, (4/06/2014). *Khartoum's partners in Beijing*, Washington DC: USA.

Freeman-Grenville, G. P. S. 1975. (Ed). *The East African Coast: Select documents from the first to the earlier nineteenth century*, Rex Collings: London.

Frick, J. (12/01/2008). 'The impact of mass culture: Family myths, beliefs and trends' in *Lebanon Daily News*.

Ganiage, J. 1985. "North Africa" Yvonne Brett (T. R.). In J. D. Fage and Roland Oliver, (eds.), *The Cambridge History of Africa*, Volume 6, Cambridge University Press: London, pp.159-171.

Gelfand, M. 1973. *The Genuine Shona: Survival Values of an African Culture*, Mambo Press: Gweru, Zimbabwe.

Geller, S. 1995. "The Colonial Era" in Africa, In Phyllis, M. Martin and Patrick, O'Meara (eds.) Bloomington: Indiana University Press.

Giddens, A. 1993. (2nd ed). *Sociology*, Polity Press: United States of America.

Gogoyo, N. (20/04/2010). Interview, Mossurizi, Manica Province, Mozambique.

Gonese, C. 1999. The three worlds, *Compas Newsletter*, (1).

Gossett, T. 1963. *Race: The history of an idea in America*, Southern Methodist University Press: Dallas.

Graber, D. 1980. *Mass Media and American Politics*, Washington DC: Congressional Quarterly Press.

Guha, R. 1997. *Dominance without hegemony: history and power in colonial India*, Cambridge, MA: Harvard University Press.

Gyekye, K. 1996. *African cultural values: An introduction*, Sankofa Publishing Company: Accra, Ghana.

Hall, E.T. 1992. *The Hidden Dimension*, New York, Anchor Books.

Hammersmith, J. A. 2007. *Converging indigenous and western knowledge systems: Implications for tertiary education*, Unpublished Doctoral Thesis, Pretoria: University of South Africa (UNISA).

Harding, S. 1994. Is science multicultural?: Challenges, resources, opportunities, uncertainties, *Configurations* 2 (2): 301-330.

Herald Newspaper, 2010. *Women charged with witchcraft in Zimbabwe: Harare*, 20/03/2010. Retrieved from: http://www.herald.co.zw/ (accessed on 22 April 2010).

Harrison, M. 1998. *The Language of Theatre*, London: Routledge.

Hochschild, A. 1998. *King Leopold's Ghost: A Story of Greed, Terror, and Heroism in Colonial Africa*, Houghton Mifflin Company: New York.

Hoole, A. 2014. Community-based conservation and protected areas: Commons perspectives for promoting biodiversity and social justice in southern Africa, In Sowman, M. and Wynberg, R. (Eds). *Governance for justice and environmental sustainability: Lessons across natural resource sectors in sub-Saharan Africa*, Earthscan Publishers, London.

Humbaraci, A. and Nicole, M. 1974. *Portugal's African Wars*, The Third Press: New York.

Ikuenobe, P. 2000. Internationalism and the Rationality of African Metaphysical Beliefs, *African Philosophy*, 13(2): 125-142.

International Conference on ADIS, 1993. Retrieved from: *http://gateway.nih.gov/* (accessed on 2 June 2010).

Jalata, A. 2013. Colonial terrorism, global capitalism and African underdevelopment: 500 years of crimes against African people, *Journal of Pan African Studies*, Vol. 5 (9): 1-43.

Jung, C. and Jon, H. ny. *Mao, the unknown story*, China Central Television: China.

Kahari, G. 1980. *The Search for Zimbabwean Identity: An Introduction to the Black Zimbabwean Novel*, Gwelo: Mambo Press.

Kahari, G. 1986. *Aspects of the Shona Novel and Other Related Genres*, Gweru: Mambo Press.

Katerere, Y. 1999. Overview of CBNRM in the region, *Paper presented at the workshop: CBNRM and its contribution to economic development in Southern Africa*, 3-5 June 1999, Chilo Safari Lodge, Mahenye: Zimbabwe.

Kiernan, Ben. 2007. *Blood and Soil: A World History of Genocide and Extermination from Sparta to Darfur*, Yale University Press: New Haven.

Kiernan, V. G. 1982. *From Conquest to Collapse: European Empires from 1815-1960*, Pantheon Books: New York.

King, M. 2012. China-Africa trade booms, *Joc.com, 18/06/2012*, (Accessed 4 July 2014).

Kothari, A. 2007. Traditional knowledge and sustainable development, *International Institute for Sustainable Development (IISD)*, Available at: http://www.iisd.org.

Kovel, J. 1970. *White racism: A psychohistory*, Random House: New York.

Lane, L. 2007.The Influence of the Media in Politics, Campaigns and Elections, *Yahoo Contributor Network*,

Available at: https://contributor.yahoo.com (Accessed on 09/04/2014).

Le Monde Diplomatique, 2005. *China's trade safari in Africa*, Ministry of Foreign Affairs of the People's Republic of China.

Linebaugh, K. and Oster, S. 2006.*Cnooc pays US$2. 27 billion for Nigerian oil, gas stake*, Wall Street Journal.

Lonsdale, J. 1985. The European scramble and conquest in African history, In J. D. And Oliver, R. (Eds). *The Cambridge History of Africa*, Volume 6, from 1870 to 1905, pp. 680-766, Cambridge University Press: Cambridge.

Magubane, B. 1996. *The making of a racist state: British imperialism and the Union of South Africa, 1875-1910*, The Red Sea Press: Trenton, New Jersey.

Makahamadze, T., Grand, N., and Tavuyanago, B. 2009. The role of traditional leaders in fostering democracy, justice and human rights in Zimbabwe, *The African Anthropologist*, Vol. 16, Nos 1&2 2009, p. 33-47.

Malaba, M. Z. 1998. "Zimbabwean literature, in Zimbabwe Council of Churches", Welcome To Zimbabwe: World Council of Churches Eighth Assembly, pp.48–9. Harare: ZCC.

Mapara, J. 2009. Indigenous Knowledge Systems in Zimbabwe: Juxtaposing Postcolonial Theory, *The Journal of Pan African Studies*, 3(1): 139-155.

Marongwe, N. 2004. Traditional authority in community-based natural resource management (CBNRM): The case of Chief Marange in Zimbabwe, In Dzingirai, V. and Breen, C. 2004. *Confronting the crisis in community conservation-Case studies from Southern Africa, Centre for Environment,* Agriculture and Development, University of KwaZulu-Natal.

Mathews, G. And Yang, Y. 2012. How Africans pursue low-end globalisation in Hong Kong and Mainland China, *Journal of Current Chinese Affairs*, pp. 1-28.

Martian2, (01/04/2013). Only China can build a China-Sudan Friendship Bridge for US$ 20 million,

Mawere, M. 2010. On Pursuit of the Purpose of Life: The Shona Metaphysical Perspective, *J. Pan African Stud.*, .3(6): 269-284.

Mawere, M. 2010b. "Peeping into the world beyond": Metaphysical speculations on the nature of life in disembodied bodies, *Educational Research*, 1(11): 568-576.

Mawere, M. 2011. Epistemological and moral implications of characterisation in African literature: A critique of Patrick Chakaipa's '*Rudo Ibofu*' (love is blind), *Journal of English and literature*, 2(1): 1-9.

Mawere, M. 2012. *The struggle of indigenous knowledge systems in an age of globalisation: A case for children's traditional games*, Langaa RPCIG, Bamenda: Cameroon.

Mawere, M. 2013. *Lyrics of reason and experience*, Langaa RPCIG, Bamenda: Cameroon.

Mawere, M. 2005. Life after Bodily Death: Myth or Reality? *The Zambezia Journal of Humanities*, 32(2): 26-46.

Mawere, M. 2014. *Environmental conservation through Ubuntu and other emerging perspectives*, Langaa RPCIG, Bamenda: Cameroon.

Mawere, M. and Kadenge, M. 2010. Zvierwa as African Indigenous Knowledge Systems: Epistemological and Ethical Implications of Selected Shona Taboos, *INDILINGA-African Journal of Indigenous Knowledge Systems*, 9 (1): 29-44.

Masolo, D. A. 1995. *African Philosophy in Search of Identity*, East African Educational Publishers: Nairobi, Kenya

Mbiti, J. S. 1975. *An Introduction to African Religion*, London: Heinemann.

Mbiti, J. 1999. *African religions and philosophy*, (2nd Ed), Heinemann, London.

McCarthy, B. K. 1991. Teaching African religions, in Juergensmeyer, M. (Ed.), *Teaching the introductory course in Religious Studies: A Sourcebook*, pp. 147–55. Atlanta: Scholars Press.

Mengara, D. M. (Ed). 2001. *Images of Africa: Stereotypes and realities*, Trenton and Asmara: Africa world Press.

Miller, J. 2002. West Africa, *In:* David. N, (Ed.).*The Atlantic Slave Trade*, 2nd Ed, Houghton Mifflin Company: Boston, pp. 45-51.

Ministry of Foreign Affairs of the People's Republic of China, *China-Africa Relations*, 25 April   2002.

Ministry of Foreign Affairs of the People's Republic of China, *China-Africa Relations*, 2009.

Mkhulisi, M. 2013. Outrage over sex ruling, In *Daily Sun* (4/10/2013), Available at: news@dailysun.co.za.

Muekalia, D.J. 2004. Africa and China's strategic partnership, *African Security Review* 13 (1): 5-11.

Mugambi JNK. 2005. *Christianity and the African cultural heritage.*; 2005.Website.

Mugambi JNK. *Rites of passage and cultural education in tropical Africa today.*; 2005.Website

Mukamuri, B. 1995. *Making sense of social forestry: A political and contextual study of forestry practices in South-central Zimbabwe*, PhD Thesis, University of Tampere: Finland.

Murombedzi, J.C. 2003. 'Pre-colonial and colonial conservation practices in Southern Africa and their legacy today', In Whande, W.; Kepe, T. and Murphree, M.W. 2003. *Local communities, enquiry and conservation in Southern Africa*, Africa Resource Trust: Harare, Zimbabwe.

Nevinson, H. 1906. *A Modern Slavery*, Haper & Brothers: London.

Nzewi, M. 2007. A contemporary study of musical arts: Informed by African Indigenous Knowledge Systems, *Volume 4 Illuminations, Reflection and Explorations*, Ciima Series.

Obbo, C. 2006. *Experiencing and understanding AIDS in Africa*, Centre of African Studies, United Kingdom.

Obioha, U. 2010. Globalisation and the future of African cultures, *Philosophical Papers and Review*, 2 (1): 1-8.

Ocholla, D. 2007. Marginalised knowledge: An agenda for indigenous knowledge development and integration with other forms of knowledge, *International Review of Information Ethics*, 7 (09): 1-10.

Ogundele, S. O. 2006. "Quest for Our Ancestors: Some Reflections on Ancient African Heritages and Contemporary Politics", in DapoAdelugba, Dan Izevbaye, and J. Egbelfie (Eds.), *Wole Soyinka at 70 Festschrift*. Place of publication not indicate. Published by *LACE Occasional Publications and Data Partners logistics Ltd.*, pp. 689-730.

Onyango-Ogutu, B. and Roscoe, A. 1974. *Keep My Words: Luo Oral Literature*, Nairobi: Heinemann.

Opoku, K. 2014. The genocide: Will Namibian bones haunt Germans forever? *The Southern Times Newspaper,* Windhoek: Namibia, (26 Jan 2014). Available at: www.southerntimesafrica.com.

Pagden, A. 1982. *The fall of natural man,* Cambridge University Press: Cambridge.

Page, B. 1996. The Mass Media as Political Actors, *Journal of Political Science and Politics,* 29 (1): 20- 24.

Pankhurst, R. 1961. *An introduction to the economic history of Ethiopia,* Lalibela House: London.

Pearsall, J. 1999. *The New Oxford Dictionary of English,* York: Oxford University Press.

Perry, A. 2008. *A Chinese colour war,* Time. (Available at Timemag_service.com).

Polanyi, K. 1944. *The Great Transformation,* Beacon Press: Boston.

Pollard, S. and Cousins, T. 2014. Legal pluralism and the governance of freshwater resources in southern Africa: Can customary governance be embedded within the statutory frameworks for integrated water resources management? In Sowman, M. and Wynberg, R. (Eds). *Governance for justice and environmental sustainability: Lessons across natural resource sectors in sub-Saharan Africa,* Earthscan Publishers, London.

Puri, S. R. 2006. 'Education – New Horizons', *A quarterly Journal of Education,* (2006 Edition), vol. Iv.

Ramose, M. B. 1999. *African philosophy through Ubuntu,* Harare: Mond Books.

Ramsden, G. 1996. Media coverage of issues and candidates: What balance is appropriate in a democracy? *Political Science Quarterly*, 111 (1): 65-81.

Ranger, T. 1985. *The Invention of Tribalism in Zimbabwe*, Mambo Press: Gweru, Zimbabwe.

Reuss, C. and Hiebert, R.E. 1985.*Impact of mass media*, Longman, Brazil.

Sapir, E. 1977.*Monograph series in language, culture and cognition*, Jupiter Press.

Schein, E.H. 1992. *Organisational culture and leadership*, San Francisco: Jossey Bass.

Schmidt, E., 1966, *Peasants, Traders and Wives: Shona Women in the History of Zimbabwe, 1870-1939*, Harare: Baobab Books.

Selebi, M. 2013. Act against racist teachers: SAHRC recommends widespread sanctions, In Sowetan Newspaper (4 Oct 2013), Available at: www.sowetanlive.co.za

Shinn, D. (2/09/2012). *China's involvement in Mozambique*, International Policy Digest.

Shutte, A. 2001.*Ubuntu: An ethic for a new South Africa*, Pietermaritzburg: Cluster Publications.

Sidane, J. 1995. Democracy in African societies and Ubuntu, *Focus* 3:3 (Nov./Dec.), 1-16.

Sithole, N. 1970. *Obed Mutezo: The Mudzimu Christian Nationalist*, Nairobi: Oxford University Press.

Siyakwazi, B. J. 1995. Church and state partnership in African education in colonial Zimbabwe, *Zimbabwe Journal of Educational Research*, 7 (3): 323–42.

Snow, P. 1988. *The Star Raft: China's encounter with Africa*, Weidenfeld and Nicholson: New York, USA.

Thoke, M. 2012. *Hard labour: Poor conditions at Chinese firms*, Southern Africa Resource Watch (SARW).

Sowetan Newspaper, (27 May 2013), 'Shame of pregnant pupils', South Africa, p. 2. Available at: www.sowetanlive.co.za.

Sowetan Newspaper, South Africa (4 Oct 2013), Available at: www.sowetanlive.co.za.

Sowman, M. and Wynberg, R. (Eds). 2014. *Governance for justice and environmental sustainability: Lessons across natural resource sectors in sub-Saharan Africa*, Earthscan Publishers, London.

Springer, E. P. 2003. Culture and consciousness: The challenge for African selfhood and identity, *Proceeding of the Indaba 2003: History and cultures in Africa: The movement of ideas, people and books*, Zimbabwe International Book Fair (ZIBF): Harare, Zimbabwe.

Stallman, R. 2009. 'The GNU Operating System, What's in a Name?', GNU Project.

Standard Newspaper, 2010. *Ngozi*: Primitive superstition or reality? Published on 23/05/2010. Retrieved from: http://www.thestandard.co.zw (accessed on 12 May 2010).

Tempels, P. 1945. *Bantu Philosophy*, Paris: Presence Africaine.

The Chronicles (08/10/2014). '2 Form Four students caught red-handed having sex in class, groaning in pleasure', *The Chronilces*, Harare: Zimbabwe. (Retrieved: 10/10/2014).

The Economist, (23/03/2013). *Africa and China: More than minerals*, Nairobi: Kenya. (Retrieved: 02 July 2014).

161

Thomson, D. China's soft power in Africa: From the 'Beijing consensus' to healthy diplomacy, ttnews=3901.

Tong, X. 2009. Sudanese-Chinese Friendship Bridge spans over Nile River, *Xinhuanews*, (03/04/2009).

Trompenaars, F. 1994. *Riding the waves of culture: Understanding cultural diversity in global business,* Irwin, New York.

Tsiko, S. 2012. 'How the West is bleeding Africa', *The Herald Newspaper*, Harare: Zimbabwe (2 August 2012).

UNESCO Report, (17/06/2009). 'Safeguarding projects for the GuleWankulu and the ChopiTimbila – Cultural Tourism', Mozambique.

Wa Thiongo, N. 1981. *Decolonising the Mind: The politics of Language in African Literature*, London: James Currey Publishers.

Webster. 1997. (Ed). *Random House Unabridged Dictionary*, Random House Inc., USA.

Wei, S. 2013. *China's perspective on the development of sub-Saharan countries*, Centre for Global Cooperation   Research, Duisburg: Germany.

Winch, P. 1970. Understanding a primitive society, In Wilson, B. (Ed.), *Rationality,* Oxford: Basil Blackwell.

Wiredu, K. 1996. *Cultural universals and particulars: An African perspective*, Indiana University Press.

Wonacott, P. 2011. *In Africa, U.S. Watches China's Rise*, The Wall Street Journal.

World Bank, 1998. *World Development Report 1998–1999: Knowledge for Development*, Washington: USA.

World Bank, 2004. *Indigenous knowledge: Local pathways to global development*, Knowledge and Learning Group Africa Region, World Bank, Available at: at http://worldbank.org/afr/ik/default.htm.

York, G. (18/07/2005). *Revisiting the history of the high seas*, The Globe and Mail.

Zhwarara, R. 1987. Zimbabwean fiction in English, *Zambezia Journal of Humanities*, 14 (2), 131–46.

www.ingramcontent.com/pod-product-compliance
Lightning Source LLC
Chambersburg PA
CBHW071027280326
41935CB00011B/1480